Here's what ot

A Deeper Walk with Jesus.

"Several years ago, the Lord prompted me to start a Bible study. When I saw that the group was growing, I needed more teachers. When I met Shelia and heard her heart, I immediately asked if she would become one of the teachers for the group. As she taught, I saw the love within her heart for the Lord. This expression of His love showed a hunger and desire to see people grow and develop in their relationship with their Heavenly Father. In this book, she shares several of her teachings that will help you to dive into the depth of living waters and discover areas of your spiritual walk you may not have known before. Allow this book, *A Deeper Walk with Jesus*, to minister to your heart."

-P. Armour, Christian Minister

"Knowing Shelia for several years and sitting in her Bible study classes, I knew that she was passionate about God and willing to share His words with the world. It's no wonder that her heartfelt message displayed in this book will change lives and show how to follow in the footsteps of Jesus. "Pappa God's Exhortation," which is my favorite part, will indeed inspire, encourage, motivate, and hopefully help people to have a closer walk with God."

-Marva Simon, CEO of Creative Mind Production LLC,
Author, Mentor, Entrepreneur

"What a pleasure it is for me to endorse Shelia Humphries' book. For the years I have known her, all I heard her talk about was getting this project started. Shelia expounds on the Word of God in such positive and profound ways; she helps the audiences in her Bible study classes to understand on every level. Through the content in this devotional, one can learn, grow, and have a great relationship with God (if so desired). Shelia is passionate about God and she is passionate about souls! I pray that as she answered the calling of God, lives will be impacted."

-Deacon Leslie Simon, Vice President of Creative Mind Production LLC, Mason—Home Remodeling Specialist, Evangelist, Speaker—Nursing Home Ministries

"Shelia and I have known each other for several years, and our hearts remain in unison to see people grow and develop in Christ. In this book, you'll see that she seriously expresses her heart through the Word of God, by the depth and understanding given. A wounded soul or unrevealed feelings that may lie deep within are exposed and highlighted through different avenues, and are brought to the surface. God desires to go deeper through these chapters that will minister to your soul. Allow this book, "A Deeper Walk with Jesus"—through the Holy Spirit—to teach you things that can't be seen."

- *LuAnn Morgan*, Graceful Women Warrior Ministries

A DEEPER WALK WITH JESUS

Lord, teach me what I cannot see

SHELIA HUMPHRIES

A DEEPER WALK WITH JESUS

Lord, teach me what I cannot see

SHELIA HUMPHRIES

Splendor Publishing

College Station, Texas

SPLENDOR PUBLISHING
Published by Splendor Publishing
College Station, TX.

First published printing, September, 2023

Bible verses from the following translations were used in this book:

THE HOLY BIBLE, NEW INTERNATIONAL VERSION®, NIV® Copyright © 1973, 1978, 1984, 2011 by Biblica, Inc.™ Used by permission. All rights reserved worldwide.

Scripture taken from the New King James Version®. Copyright © 1982 by Thomas Nelson. Used by permission. All rights reserved.

Scripture quotations marked TPT are from The Passion Translation®. Copyright © 2017, 2018, 2020 by Passion & Fire Ministries, Inc. Used by permission. All rights reserved. ThePassionTranslation.com.

Scripture quotations taken from the Amplified® Bible (AMP), Copyright © 2015 by The Lockman Foundation. Used by permission. lockman.org.

Scripture quotations marked KJV are from the King James Version of the Bible in the Public Domain.

Library of Congress Control Number: 2023914326
A Deeper Walk with Jesus: Lord, Teach Me what I Cannot See
Self Help
1. Religion
2. Spirituality

Cover image: 177791239 © Josephine Julian Lobijin Dreamstime.com

ISBN: 978-1-940278-26-1

Printed in the United States of America.

For more information about this book, or to order bulk copies of this book for events, seminars, conferences, or training, please contact the author.

Dedication

This book is dedicated to some very special people: those who have begun a journey to know and love the Lord, Jesus. It is my prayer and desire that you come to experience the depth and breadth of His great love for you as you follow Him each day of your life. His love never fails.

Contents

Lord, teach me what I cannot see.

Foreword

I am a devotional reader. It is my favorite kind of reading. There is not a more important kind of book! And the most important kind of devotional is one that helps us "draw closer" to God. It is perhaps the most ambitious type of effort to think that you could possibly help someone in the most important relationship they can have: their relationship with God!

Our Lord has created for us the possibility of a life above all others. In this book, Shelia Humphries has created a series of touching invitations to enter higher realms, toward a Heavenly spiritual life.

Each invitation is completed with a personal address from "Pappa God," who longs for us to experience ever deeper avenues of His love and care. Then, she caps off each devotional reading by giving us probing questions to consider. In the process, she offers solid, scriptural help to lead us into our own continuing, "deeper" study.

Shelia knows that some earthly fathers failed their children, but our Heavenly Father never does. Her vision of "Pappa" paints a warm, strong, image of God as an intimate, loving parent: a parent who never fails His children. In this light, Shelia sows the seed and prays that eyes are opened and ears hear the voice of the Father, in hopes that they will discover and experience this loving Heavenly Father's strength, care, and comfort.

In the beginning of chapter eight, Shelia states that, "The responsibility of redressing our damaged soul with the fruit of God's character is an honor." Embracing this honor is the primary duty of each serious servant of God. In this devotional workbook, Shelia gives us vision of the nature of this primary duty, and offers guidance not only for what to do, but also, *how* to do it.

To Shelia, Jesus is her everything and *that* is the bright aim of this book! Stand strong and believe that when you apply these principles, they will transform you. Shelia gives you tools and steps to make God *your* everything, too.

Shelia describes this closer walk with Christ as feeling like the "Coat of Love" you never want to take off—an intimacy with God that wraps you in warmth, security, and a love which will never leave nor forsake you. It is a true divine unity when you and God become one. He's in you and you're in Him. Shelia offers you this many-colored coat of love to help you feel the Father's care and goodness. Her work is sure to be a heartwarming boost to your spiritual life and strength. I suggest you give *A deeper Walk with Jesus* a reverent reading.

Tim G. Carter, aka, "Seek"
Pastor and Founder of Dear Life Ministries,
Author of *Positive X Positive = Unlimited*,
Thomasville, North Carolina

Introduction

Having served the Lord for several years in Alabama, it was time for a change. The desire for Bible college was heavy on my heart, while the need for me to care for my parents was pressing.

After the passing of my parents, and my house sold, it was time for college. As a student, I appreciated the families who welcomed me into their homes. Although living with others was tiresome, I soon became restless with the moves, even though I saw that God had other reasons for this journey. Not returning to Alabama, God began a new adventure for me in Texas. Although, planting new roots in another state took time and patience.

Fast forward a few years: still having to live with families, early retirement was just around the corner, and looked really good. Excitement kept my eyes focused on having my own home.

When I moved into my own apartment and finally settled, the Lord began to press upon my heart to teach. Having taught in the past, a hunger to use this gift wouldn't leave.

After meeting many of the residents, I attended a Bible study within the apartment complex and was soon asked to teach. When Covid stole our freedom to fellowship, I started my own Bible study in my apartment. For the next three and a half years, I led "A Deeper Fellowship" in Biblical and discipleship lessons.

When one hundred lessons were taught, the Lord told me it was time for a break. This was the time that the Lord spoke to me to put these lessons in a book. I have condensed these lessons for the book with prophetic exhortations from the Father. Questions are given for your self-help study and to use for Bible study groups and discussions.

Take this time to hear what the Father is saying and learn to apply His Word for *A Deeper Walk with Jesus*. I hope you enjoy this new journey as I have in writing His words.

Shelia

Chapter 1

Do You Wear His Coat?

"He will cover you with his feathers, and under
his wings you will find refuge; his faithfulness
will be your shield and rampart."
(Psalm 91:4 NIV)

Years ago, I had the privilege to minister in a girl's correctional center. As a way of sharing what the Lord had done in their lives, the girls created a book of testimonies and poems. One of them had authored a short poem about the coat that she loved to wear. It was a warm, blue coat and she called it her "Coat of Love." Every time she put this coat on, she had a feeling of being loved, and that was her protection. She never wanted to take it off. It was a blanket of warmth and love that gave her a sense of security that seemed to say, "I will never leave you." She wouldn't let it out of her sight.

I pondered on this short poem with tears running down my face, knowing that Jesus was my coat. His love covers and protects me, promising never to leave. However, a moment of sadness touched my heart, as I pondered that many people are lonely and don't know of this love—this Jesus. So please allow me to share Him with you.

The above verse lets us know that Jesus will cover us with His feathers, and under His wings is our refuge. This is His coat of love, and His faithfulness will be a shield and rampart, our protection. As long as we stay connected to Him, the Vine (as stated in the Bible in John 15:1-8), we are fed with the nourishment that is needed.

I love this verse of scripture: "Taste and see that the Lord is good" (Psalm 34:8 NIV). Opportunities are given to us every day to taste of God's goodness, yet we don't always step out in faith and receive from Him. Even if a coat of love, security, and warmth were given to us, questions of doubt from the enemy would present themselves. Questions such as, "Where did it come from," or, "Is it safe to put on?" could turn into apprehensive feelings of fear. But, just as we need a coat in the winter, we need this man named Jesus.

Why? He is a man that will never leave you nor forsake you. He doesn't condemn, always forgives, loves unconditionally, and died on the cross for your sins. Like the coat, He's worth putting on and testing out the fit, by trusting and believing in Him. When you taste of His goodness, you'll never want to be out from under His wings of love. You will hunger to always be connected to Him, with the warmth of His love and protection.

The coat of His love is to always be worn, never taken off. Like a mother bird protects her children under her feathers or wings, so our Lord Jesus protects us. If you have not put on this coat of love, I challenge you today to receive from Him. You will find refuge and His faithfulness in the coat of His love.

Pappa God's Exhortation

Allow Me to show My love to you so that you can taste and see of My goodness. My faithfulness and promises will protect you all the days of your life. I will wrap My love around you so you'll never want to slip away . . . away into the desert land where death has a place to capture. So, learn of My teachings with love, for there is no one like Me. With joy from My heart, I gladly give My wings like a comforting coat, to shield and protect My love within your heart. *~Pappa God*

1. Since your salvation experience, do you feel like you are wrapped in the Father's love, as though you are wearing a coat? Explain how.

2. Compared to His feathers or wings (as expressed in Psalm 91:4), do you feel protected and covered? Do you have a coat or garment that makes you feel safe and secure? Explain your feelings.

3. Have you tasted of God's goodness? In what ways does the Father show His goodness to you and how often do you have these experiences?

4. Explain your encounters of God's goodness when trials and bad times are in your midst? Give detailed experiences.

5. If you have never had these experiences with Jesus, have you made Him Lord of your life? My friend, this is a great time to examine your heart to see whether or not you have received Jesus as Lord. Deuteronomy 30: 19-20 describes that life and

death is set before us, but tells us to choose life. Don't let this day pass by without knowing that eternal life awaits you.

6. What did you learn from Pappa God's exhortation?

> Have you shared with others how Jesus has touched your heart, explaining how His love makes you feel protected, warm, and loved? If not, make it a goal to share with someone about His love.

Notes of Reflection: _____

Chapter 2

How Do I Receive Salvation?

"Jesus answered and said to him, 'Most assuredly,
I say to you, unless one is born again, he cannot
see the kingdom of God.'"
(John 3:3 NKJV)

In the beginning, when God created the heavens and the earth, He also created man. As time went on, after the fall of Adam and Eve, man had no eternal direction, but because of His love, God sent His only Son to die for our sins. Think about it! Who would give up their son to die for you? Love! True love! A love you'll never find, except through God.

When God chose a redemption plan for His creation, the Word—the second person of the Trinity—became flesh. Jesus, God's Son, walked through this earth, teaching, healing, and demonstrating the miracles of His Father's love. His assignment was complete when He died on the cross at Calvary and was raised from the dead, three days later. Now, He sits at the right hand of His Father, on His throne.

So, how do I receive this love, or this man named Jesus into my life? Jesus tells us, "'unless one is born again, he cannot see the kingdom of God'" (John 3:3 NKJV). In that same passage of scripture, Nicodemus asked Jesus how it was possible to return to your mother's womb. Jesus replied, "'unless one is born of water and the Spirit, he cannot enter the kingdom of God'" (John 3:5 NKJV).

When we give Christ the invitation to come into our hearts and be Lord, permission is granted for change to begin.

To receive a rebirth is to die to the old nature. "I have been crucified with Christ; it is no longer I who live, but Christ lives in me; and the life which I now live in the flesh I live by faith in the Son of God, who loved me and gave Himself for me" (Galatians 2:20 NKJV: this verse is explained in full in chapter four). Our old spirit nature of the flesh dies and we become new in Christ. He fills our heart with a comfort of His Agape love, promising never to leave nor forsake us.

As we hunger for more of His presence (through reading the Word), the scripture shows us who we are to become in Christ. Because of our love for Him, we allow change to come and death to our fleshly ways. So, as we move forward to our next step of *A Deeper Walk with Jesus*, we will learn that our commitment becomes a sacrifice.

Pappa God's Exhortation

This day, I knock upon the door of your heart, to give you an opportunity to put on My coat of love that I freely give to you. My Word (Rhema, Logos) is the solid rock foundation of My Kingdom. My Word (the Bible) or the Logos, speaks of the steps you must take to receive eternity. The choice is yours to make. When you accept My Son, Jesus, as your Savior, Lord, and friend, you are forgiven and set free from the death penalty that awaited you. My Holy Spirit will lead and guide you each step of the day to accomplish the destiny I have designed for your life. You are the apple of My eye and in Me you can do ALL things when you call upon My name. Make this day your day of salvation by being born into My Spirit, to live eternally in My Kingdom. *~Pappa God*

1. What was your response to "you must be born again?"

2. Did you think like Nicodemus? Explain.

3. Did you ever think that God's Son, Jesus, loved us enough to die for every soul on the face of this earth? Explain why you may have thought that He couldn't love you enough to die on a cross.

4. Can you say without a doubt that you believe He died for you? How can you explain this and how would you share this experience with others?

5. Do you deserve that love? Why do you think He would love a sinner like you? Are you at peace knowing He lives within you?

6. What did you learn from Pappa God's exhortation?

_____

_____

> "Behold, now is the accepted time; behold, now is the day of salvation." (2 Corinthians 6:2 NKJV)

Notes of Reflection: _____

Chapter 3

Commitment is a Sacrifice

"And the king of Israel answered and said, 'My
lord, O king, just as you say, I and all that I
have are yours.'"
(1 Kings 20:4 NKJV)

Behind the wedding vows between a man and a woman is
the commitment and sacrifice of "for better or worse." Many
anxious-to-say-"I-do" couples are often surprised to find that
the wedding rings and vows become empty. On top of that, the
entrustment of the words, "I will never leave you regardless
of the circumstances," can easily become broken promises.

Although our commitment with Jesus is similar, one thing
is different: His Word promises that He will never leave
nor forsake us (Hebrews 13:5). But. . . has our relationship
with God the Father, Jesus, and the Holy Spirit become weak
and uncommitted? With this kind of indecisiveness and
uncertainty, how do we secure our spiritual commitment
of love for our Savior?

As we submerge ourselves in the Word of God, the truth
and His Agape love will continue to open our eyes. Our love
and faith for Him starts to deepen as we see the love that
Jesus has for His Father. God gave His only son, Jesus, who
sacrificed His life for us, because of His love and His obedience
to His Father (John 3:16). The Lord seeks within our hearts
the same desire to please Him and obey His commandments,
because of our love for Him.

Romans 12: 1-3 gives to us several key points: (1) present our bodies as a living sacrifice, (2) one that is holy, and (3) one that is acceptable to God. Then, Paul (the writer of Romans) outlines how this can be done: (1) do not be conformed to this world but be transformed by the renewing of your mind, and (2) that you may prove what is that good, acceptable, and perfect will of God.

In order for these points to be accomplished in our life, we have to die to our ways. In 1 Corinthians 15:31, Paul tells us that he dies daily! In Romans 8:13, the Word tells us that if we live according to the flesh we will die, but if by the Spirit we put to death the deeds of the body, we will live.

Saying "No" to an ungodly character or lifestyle, and/or walking away from the old into the new, is a sacrifice. Allowing Christ to have permission to remake you into His likeness is a journey that involves sacrifice and a commitment to Him. This walk is not a road filled with red roses. The valleys that teach and prune us can get rough at moments. Dying to the flesh is not a fun process. However, knowing that Christ is committed to you, the walk through the valleys can become a blessing.

In order to have a successful, committed relationship to God, sacrifice is necessary. The "all about me" mentality no longer exists. Your marriage with Jesus is always first!

When the wedding vows were exchanged with "I do," the "me" dies. The two become one, and death comes to the individual self. The "what about me" has died. Once again, giving up your flesh for the ways of God is a committed sacrifice. All that I have is yours.

Pappa God's Exhortation

When I first created you, I married you, with a love that would never depart. Sometimes, unaware that it was My love that blessed and forgave you, without thanks, you hardened your heart. But My arms are always open and My ears are always ready to hear the cry of your voice saying, Pappa, are you near? Yes, My child, I told you I would never leave nor forsake the marriage vow I gave. I sent My son, Jesus, to prepare the way. The marriage supper still awaits you as long as you have forsaken the world and its call. Daily I seek your hand, so I can connect the marriage band, always looking for a committed bride of sacrifice. ~*Pappa God*

1. Did you ever think that your commitment with Jesus was like a marriage between a man and a woman?

2. What do you think the wedding vows mean between two people?

3. How would you associate these vows or this commitment with Jesus? Explain.

4. What does the word *sacrifice* mean to you? Is *sacrifice* different than *obedience*? How? Read 1 Samuel 15:20-23 and John 14:15 and explain.

5. Can you make a sacrifice of a lifetime commitment to Jesus? Would this sacrifice be made out of your love toward Him, which involves being obedient to Him? In John 14:23, Jesus tells us that if we love Him we will obey Him.

6. Jesus said He will never leave nor forsake you. Does your commitment to Him say the same thing? Will you or have you left your commitment? Does obedience have something to do with your decision?

_____

_____

7. What did you learn from Pappa God's exhortation?

> "Then he took the Book of the Covenant and read in the hearing of the people. And they said, 'All that the Lord has said we will do, and be obedient.'" (Exodus 24:7 NKJV)

Notes of Reflection: _____

Chapter 4

What about Me? (Part 1)

"I have been crucified with Christ; it is no longer I
who live, but Christ lives in me; and the life which I
now live in the flesh I live by faith in the Son of God,
who loved me and gave Himself for me."
(Galatians 2:20 NKJV)

In the above verse, Paul shares that we were crucified with
Jesus on the cross. Although we did not die a physical death on
the cross with Him, we were on His heart. Because of His love,
His purpose was to pay the debt of our sins so that we could
live eternally with Him. Though we live in the flesh, this death
(on the cross with Jesus) represents the carnal spirit that has
died. Now, our spirit has become a new creature in Christ,
which was created in His image, though our soul still remains
with its fleshly ways, and must die.

In 1 Corinthians 15:31 (NKJV), the Apostle Paul writes, "I
die daily." Paul faced death every day when he encountered
the "wild beasts in Ephesus" (verse 32) who were evil and
against the resurrection—those who set out to corrupt the good
manners and morals of character. They were determined to
deceive and mislead.

Satan comes to steal, kill, and destroy, and his constant
attempts to corrupt never end. Our fleshly sin nature continues
to fall into the temptation of evil, unless the flesh is dealt with.
In order for a true alignment in Christ to take place, the body
and soul must walk in conjunction with the newborn spirit.

The "me, myself, and I" mentality, which is produced by the self or the soul, states that it's *my* mind, *my* will, and *my* emotions. But the Word of God lets us know that the character and fruit of the Holy Spirit is not the same as the ways of the deadly soul of self. In His Spirit, you will find the character of *His* mind, *His* will, and *His* emotions, not that of the carnal nature. We find the fruit of His Spirit in Galatians 5:22: love, joy, peace, longsuffering, kindness, goodness, faithfulness, gentleness, and self-control.

These attributes of Jesus are of a Godly nature; however, every person has been given their own character, which displays these fruits in diverse ways to others. You walk in your joy, your love, etc. But when you die to your ways, and receive His ways, you now walk in *His* character. The process of dying to the self can be difficult at times because the flesh is stubborn, rebellious, and doesn't want to change. Even when our heart desires to change, our flesh will fight until it wins the battle.

Only scratching the surface of this needed but unwanted subject, we must continue to discuss it. As we delve more into the Word, we see that dying to the self is necessary if our desire is to look like Him. Our life is not ours anymore, it belongs to Jesus; therefore, the "what about me" attitude, must die.

Pappa God's Exhortation

As I am light and there is no darkness within, the soul of self cannot live within me. It must die. My Spirit grieves and is limited for what I purpose to do in your life, because of this restriction. You are created in My likeness to imitate My character. My character is developed when you sacrifice your ways for My holy way. In Me you live and will have your being. The destiny and purpose that I designed for you will come forth when death to the carnal ways of life are left at the cross of transformation. ~*Pappa God*

1. Galatians 5:20 states that we have been crucified with Jesus. What does that mean to you?

2. How do we "walk out" a spiritual death on the cross? What does this look like in your daily walk with Jesus?

3. When Paul said that he "died daily," was he talking about a physical or a spiritual death? Read Romans 8:13 and explain what it communicates to you.

4. When the words, "me, myself, and I" are spoken, what does that mean to you? Do you believe that the "me, myself, and I" attitude is of the flesh or of the spirit?

5. How do you die to the "me, myself, and I" mentality? Read and explain John 7:17-18 and 1 John 1:5-10. Do these verses start to describe the ways and the self-will of the flesh instead

of the ways of God? Do you think we need to die to these things? Why?

_____

_____

6. What did you learn from Pappa God's exhortation?

_____

_____

> The "me, myself, and I" mentality is of the soulish area of the *will*. Pride and vanity are named as being a part of the self-righteousness of the carnal man.

Notes of Reflection: _____

Chapter 5

What about Me? (Part 2)

"Therefore, be imitators of God as dear children."
(Ephesians 5:1 NKJV)

In our last lesson, "What About Me? (Part 1)," the Apostle Paul shared in 1 Corinthians 15:31, that he died daily. Realizing that a physical death was impossible, the fleshly soul of "what about me"—an ungodly character—must die. It is impossible to imitate Jesus when our soul continues to walk in the ways of the world, pleasing ourselves. Therefore, in order to break these habits of flesh, we must seek the Holy Spirit for scripture to guide us in these changes. As we research what the Word says about the mind of Christ, His will, and His emotions, we can clearly see that our soul is not in alignment with Him.

The first element of the soul is *the mind*. We have the mind of Christ (1 Corinthians 2:16). Why? Because we are created in His likeness. His mind is His heart (Philippians 2:5-6). David had a mind like God's because his thoughts were God's thoughts, and he had a heart like God's because of his compassion and care for people.

Walking in God's *will* is the second element of the soul. When we met Jesus at the cross, we decided to follow Him and to receive *all* of Him. Therefore, we died to our ways only to consume His nature. Ephesians 5:17 (NKJV) says, "Therefore do not be unwise, but understand what the will of the Lord is." When we seek and have done His will, we will receive the promise (Hebrews 10:36).

And the third element of the soul is *emotions*. Fleshly emotions scream loudly, demanding their way, and *now*. "Help me," is usually a cry that shouts, but pride will block the answer from being received. Pride speaks over the still small voice of the Lord, causing His words not to be heard. A damaged or wounded soul causes the emotions to exert themselves. Crying out to be heard through these ungodly emotions only deepens the hole. However, this allows the Holy Spirit to highlight these areas, where death is needed. An invitation to change has occurred. Acting upon this invite will allow the soul to align with the new spirit that has been born.

When I allowed the Holy Spirit to highlight my ungodly characteristics, I saw my face in the mirror instead of His. No one except Him could have shown me the ugliness and ungodliness of who I was, with love and mercy, as He did. Giving the Holy Spirit permission to unclothe my soul was to see that death to the carnal, was needed.

When the spiritual mirror shows who we are, Jesus our model seems impossible. However, nothing is impossible knowing the Father made us in His image. Unfolding the instructions of His Word during this journey of transformation, can be tedious. Waiting to see change occur can be lengthy at times, and can cause discouragement within our heart.

As Jesus said to the disciples when they set sail out in the Sea of Galilee, "Let us cross over to the other side" (Mark 4:35 NKJV). This encouraging word is to assure you that you are going to the other side. Change is possible and can be accomplished. Let's allow the Holy Spirit to focus upon more key issues in our next lesson.

Pappa God's Exhortation

My children, don't be fooled. The enemy has blinded the eyes of the unbelievers, so people need to see with evidence, who you say you are. If you say you are a Christian, then you must be Christ-like in all your ways. Rebirth cannot happen until there is death. New wine cannot be put in old wine skins; therefore, all things must be made new. To be an imitator of Me, change must occur. I am light and there is no darkness within Me. Trust Me to make this transition within you and I will take you to the other side. *~Pappa God*

1. What does the word *imitate* mean, and how do you walk imitating someone?

2. Ephesians 5:1 tells us to be imitators of God, as beloved children. Can you imitate God's ways when you are walking in your will?

3. What do you think is the best way to imitate God? Are we to imitate Jesus in everything or only in what we want to change?

4. Can you walk in your way and expect to receive God's way of results? When James talks about being double-minded, he says not to expect anything from God (James 1:7). What do you think about that? Explain.

5. If you saw a movie of your life, heard your voice, your words, and could see your actions and character, would you see God's ways?

6. How important is it to walk in the will of God verses in your ways? Does this change in life involve dying to the flesh, as we spoke of in the last chapter?

7. What did Jesus mean when He said, "We are going to the other side?" Explain.

8. What did you learn from Pappa God's exhortation?

A mirror will only reflect what is in front of it. Another face will not be shone unless it stands behind or to the side of you. Seeing many faces shows that you are not focused only on Jesus. If you are seeing your face, the picture of carnality still shows. The picture of Jesus is the only face that you and others should see. Reflect Jesus!

Notes of Reflection: _____

Chapter 6

Put to Death

"For to me, to live is Christ, and to die is gain."
(Philippians 1:21 NKJV)

As we discussed in the previous lessons of "What About Me," the "me, myself, and I" mentality and its ungodly fruit becomes a hidden agenda that Satan uses. The phrase "put to death" in Colossians 3:5a (NKJV), indicates that something must die. The remainder of this verse informs us that it is "your members which are on the earth." But who and what are these members? The compartments of the soul, (mind, will, and emotions) have meshed with the god of darkness. Because of indulgence to sins of the flesh (fornication, uncleanness, passion, evil desire, and covetousness), spoken of in 5b, God's wrath will be executed. These sins are of the will, and doors will continue to open when you deliberately practice them.

Having shared with you the three elements of the soul, a good example about the will is in Romans 1:19-22a. They knew God; therefore, they had no excuse not to obey Him. But they did not glorify Him nor were they thankful, so God gave them over to their depraved minds. The true hearts of these men were exposed when they deliberately obeyed their own flesh instead of the truth that was before them. God's attributes and power was visible. They did not acknowledge God's creation, and their foolish hearts were darkened.

So how do we put to death the ungodly will of our flesh?

Years ago, in my third year of being a new Christian, I disobeyed the Word of the Lord, which caused me to walk away from Him. His words were to warn me of the steps ahead. The Lord was detailed about what was going to happen if I didn't obey. I chose not to believe God, and I compromised and stayed where I was. I deliberately did what I wanted to do, and God's words became reality. This one time disobedience cost me twenty years in the world. It opened new doors to the enemy. When I returned back home to the Lord, I quickly learned that obedience in His will is always first. Walking in my ways had to die.

As we have explored in the Word, our will does not fit in the new wine skin of being Christ-like. We must die to our selfish ways. It is no longer about us. It's about Christ in us. Are you willing to "put to death" the "me, myself, and I" for life in Christ? If so, let's look further into the book of Colossians to understand what Paul is talking about when he says to "put off," which is associated with our will.

Pappa God's Exhortation

I have made a way for your escape from the world, but many of you don't respond to My call. And just knowing of My name does not open the gates to glory. It is accepting My crucifixion, where you are on the cross with Me. But, born into the sin of this world, you must die to the bondage that has captured you. You must die to the darkness within. I am light and there is no darkness in Me. Darkness cannot enter the pearly gates of heaven. *~Pappa God*

1. What does this verse in Philippians 1:21 mean when life is gained through death, or to live in Christ when we have died?

2. What does the phrase "put to death" in Colossians 3:5a mean? Besides what the Bible says in this verse, can you think of some areas in your life that need to be put to death? They need to die in order for you to move on.

3. Now let's dig a little deeper: can you think of other areas in your life that need to be put to death in order for you to move on to your future?

4. When you are doing this act of "putting to death," what are you doing? What are you substituting in its place?

5. How does this help you spiritually? What do you gain?

6. Is a sacrifice involved in this process of dying to the flesh?

_____

_____

7. What did you learn from Pappa God's exhortation?

_____

_____

> Putting to death fleshly ways is like the seed buried in the dirt, to die when it is sown. "Foolish one, what you sow is not made alive unless it dies." (1 Corinthians 15:36 NKJV)

Notes of Reflection: _____

Chapter 7

Put Off

"But now you yourselves are to put off all
these: anger, wrath, malice, blasphemy, filthy
language out of your mouth."
(Colossians 3:8 NKJV)

The emotional expressions, mentioned in the above verse, are associated with our will, or the character of self that we have chosen to wear. These attitudes that shape our character are not the characteristics that Galatians 5:22 expresses to us. After being created in His image, man disobeyed and sinned against God; therefore, this perfected likeness of Christ took on a sin nature. Now the emotional language of the flesh blatantly reveals the difference between God's character and man's, through these expressions, and more.

The fruit of the Spirit in Galatians shows the purity of His characteristics. An example is love. His love will never leave nor forsake us, and it is unconditional. However, our love may appear to be like His, but when challenged, we fail. The remaining fruit mentioned in Galatians should enlighten our eyes to whom we should imitate. When we see that our walk and talk do not mimic His ways, change must occur.

In my example in the previous chapter, "Put to Death," the Lord quickened my heart to pride. I disobeyed and compromised when God spoke to me about the solution to the dilemma; I continued to walk in my will. After twenty years away from the Lord, I renewed my faith and learned that the temptations of the flesh had to be "put to death." However, this process was only a step toward walking in His image, as Ephesians 5:1 teaches. Putting off (Colossians 3:8) the ungodly character and pride of the "me, myself, and I" mentality, must take place. These attitudes and emotional feelings are fleshly. They are not the character of Christ. The attitudes listed in Colossians are expressions that have originated through another entry way. When the Holy Spirit highlights the open doors that have stirred these emotions, they become our responsibility. At that point we must learn to eliminate, or "put off" these ungodly characteristics.

After our flesh and the carnality of the soul are "put to death" and "put off," a step is necessary to fill the void. That step is "putting on" Christ. In our next lesson, we'll learn how to put on Christ in our life, which is part of the solution to these un-Christ-like character emotions.

Pappa God's Exhortation

I always provide a door of opportunity for My sheep to walk through. Open doors will lead to the destiny I have prepared for them when one steps upon My feet to walk in My will. If not, they will never receive. Many have lost this opportunity I give because of their flesh that rules far greater than their love for Me. I loved you enough to die for your sins but are you willing to die to your fleshly ways for Me? I hand to you new wine that can't be put in an old wine skin. The weight of the blessings and the open doors will destroy the old wine skin of flesh. Today is the day to break open the alabaster box by "putting off" the old man and "putting on" new life.
~ *Pappa God*

1. The last chapter's "put to death" is closely related to "put off" in this chapter. How would you explain the difference between the two?

2. What are some areas in your life that need to be "put off" verses "put to death?"

3. Before you "put off" do you "put to death?" Explain.

4. How would you explain what is within a person, verses what is on the surface of one's life that is seen? Explain.

5. Which areas need to be "put to death" or "put off"? Which of these shows that a root needs to be extracted and destroyed? Explain.

6. Although the words from Pappa God's exhortation are about opportunity, how would you connect His words to "put off"? Explain.

7. What did you learn from Pappa God's exhortation?

Have you destroyed the old wine skin of sins by "putting off," so that the new wine skin can hold all that God desires to pour into your life?

Notes of Reflection: _____

Chapter 8

Putting On

"Therefore, as the elect of God, holy and beloved, put
on tender mercies, kindness, humility, meekness,
longsuffering; bearing with one another, and forgiving
one another, if anyone has a complaint against another;
even as Christ forgave you, so you also must do."
(Colossians 3:12-13 NKJV)

The responsibility of redressing our damaged soul with the
fruit of God's character is an honor. As we choose to "put off"
those ungodly idiosyncrasies, we also make a choice to "put on"
the character of God. As the elect of God, who are holy and the
beloved of Christ, the image must be Jesus. A favorite song of
mine from years ago by Joy Williams, was "Do They See Jesus
in Me?" This song should stir our hearts with a desire and
hunger for the world to see Christ within us.

So how do we "put on" Jesus? The answer to this question is
simple. As we have disgusted in previous chapters, applying
our time to the Word and also to prayer unlocks the doors for
freedom and victory. Conviction begins to stir our hearts
concerning who we are not. When we allow the words of Christ
to create a hunger, our love towards Him should increase our
desire to change. As we draw closer to God, this fellowship
with Him becomes sweeter and our relationship deepens as
we become the image of Christ.

Satan and his demons tremble when the name of Jesus is
spoken. Therefore, the more we "put on" Jesus in our life, the
more they tremble and lessen their torment. Our desire to serve

and obey the Father—instead walking in the old sinful nature— is true repentance. Our minds should "feast on all the treasures of the heavenly realm and fill your thoughts with heavenly realities, and not with the distractions of the natural realm" (Colossians 3:2 TPT).

As I shared in the last lesson, when I returned home after twenty years in the world, the enemy did not flee automatically. The enemy refused to be bothered by my prayers, fasting, reading, and obeying the Word. Eventually, those demons learned that I refused to bow my knee to them. Daily I spoke the Word over myself with declarations and decrees. Standing on the Word, and knowing that He that is in me is greater than he who is in the world, I did not give up (Galatians 6:9)! Soon, Satan realized that my feet were planted on a solid foundation of the love of Christ.

Do you remember what the Centurion said to Jesus? "I believe; help my unbelief" (Mark 9:24 NKJV). Sometimes, we're unable to see the old man dying and a new character beginning. But all things are possible. God strips away the layers of ungodly character to reach your true identity. As each layer is removed, death occurs to those old fleshly ways, making room for the likeness of Christ. He is our model. So, as we trust Him by stepping out and becoming a doer, we start to see the newness of His characteristics appear.

Next, we'll discuss the last step, "Putting on Love," of the series, "What About Me?"

Pappa God's Exhortation

Although I strip the bad leaves from the vine, I do not leave the tree bare. New growth appears when the correct nourishment is provided. The same applies to My children. When I remove the bad from your lives, I give to you what is necessary for new spiritual growth. But it is your responsibility to take these keys and apply them. My Holy Spirit is within you to teach and guide you. It's time to put on My character and die to the old man that was crucified with Me on the cross. *~Pappa God*

1. The phrase "put on" sounds like the coat that was put on in the first chapter that protected the young girl. What is Christ talking about when He uses these words in Colossians 3:12-13?

2. How can you associate these words with your life? Do they pertain to how you walk in life as a Christian?

3. How would you make the connection of the words "put on" with the previous chapters discussed?

4. Have you started to make changes in your life? If so, share how you have "put to death," "put off," and "put on" change in your life. Describe.

5. What did you learn from Pappa God's exhortation?

When we asked God to change us, He said He will. So don't complain about how He does it; just do what He says. You'll see the old fall away and the new will blossom into its beautiful form.

Notes of Reflection: _____

Chapter 9

Putting on Love

"But above all these things put on love, which is
the bond of perfection. And let the peace of God
rule in your hearts, to which also you were called
in one body; and be thankful."
(Colossians 3:14-15 NKJV)

As I shared in the first lesson "Do You Wear His Coat," I described God's love like the wings of a bird. These feathers or wings, protect and shield from severe weather, falling objects, and wind. His love is like wearing a coat that brings comfort and safety. His presence and His character covers us like the feathers of a snow-white dove. When we "put His love on," we sacrifice our life by dying to the soul of the flesh, for more of His sweet love.

God is Love. This is His nature, His being. This verse in Colossians 3:14-15 shows that His love is a bond of perfection. Since Jesus knew no sin, He is perfect. The bond of His love— or perfect love—stands between our sin and death. Because of His love, the steps of transformation become easier to endure along the journey.

But how can you "put on" or give love when it hasn't been received? How can you forgive your enemy when you don't feel forgiven? It's hard to give away something you don't have. The "putting on" process of His character is necessary. Putting on His love is a step that can't be done correctly if you've never received His love. To love and forgive someone of their wrong against you or someone else, is an impossible task in the fleshly heart. But because we are walking in the Agape Love of God, it is possible.

When a true commitment and sacrifice has been made to Him, death to the fleshly ways occurs. We begin to walk in His perfect love because of His love toward us. We begin to experience how His perfect love eliminates fear, and peace begins to stabilize our walk.

In 1John (NIV), he gives to us the phrase, "this is how we know." When the coat of His love—which is genuine Agape Love—is seen, people know. The fruit of His Spirit begins to become dominant in our life. We walk in obedience, talk like Him, think like Him, and allow His Word to change us. We learn to forgive, seek first the kingdom of God, and we've repented and walked away from our sin. We began to see the bad change into the good, and the ungodly character shaken off. We start to put on His nature and watch His love cover a multitude of sins.

Pappa God's Exhortation

As you continue this journey up the ladder, and allow the Holy Spirit to teach you, you'll begin to embrace a deeper walk in My love. From the beginning of time, I have loved you. I created you in My image and have offered *all* of Me to you. But now its time to wear My character by taking off the old—or dying to the flesh—and putting on the fruit of My Spirit. These attributes of who I am will give you favor and blessings because you desire to walk in Me. So, know and listen to My voice, and walk in My ways. Refusing to put on My love is rebelling against the words of My love, which is My Word. Don't be fooled: I know when your love is sincere and you desire to have *all* of Me. ~*Pappa God*

1. Did we not *receive* love when we first accepted Jesus as Lord of our life? We *received* love, so now it's easier to give love, but death to the old, sinful man must take place first. Explain how the old, sinful man has died and how you have "put on" God's love.

2. God takes us out of Egypt (our hell), but Egypt needs to be taken out of us. This is the dying process. During this sanctification period, we learn how to die to the flesh in order to put on—or wear—His love. Explain how God is taking Egypt out of you.

3. When God's love is oozing out of us, we can't help but love in His Agape love. Do you walk in His Love but still experience fleshly emotions that attack? Do you act out in a rage or in an ungodly way? Or, do you press through and walk in love? How do you press through to walk in love?

4. Does it take you a long time to forgive others, or are you quick to forgive?

5. His Word says that love covers a multitude of sins. Is your flesh quick to explode, or do you purpose to walk in God's love? Explain how God is teaching you to "put on" His love through these opportunities?

6. Forgiveness is a big step. Walking in His love is a big step when you need to forgive. What must you do to "put on" His love when you have unforgiveness?

7. What did you learn from Pappa God's exhortation?

> The Love of the Father is an everlasting love with no conditions attached. It is unconditional love. If He tells us to be imitators of Him as little children, can your love toward others be unconditional?

Notes of Reflection: _____

Chapter 10

The Fight

"The thief does not come except to steal, and to kill,
and to destroy. I have come that they may have life,
and they may have it more abundantly."
(John 10:10 NKJV)

In the previous chapter, "Putting on Love," you learned to live in God's Agape Love by dying to the carnal ways, and in doing so you became a target to the enemy. As we walk in God's ways, Satan doesn't like it. As the verse above states, Satan comes to steal, kill, and destroy. The Christian is his main target to destroy! Anything that Satan can use to destroy eternal life, he will suggest to us.

The book of Genesis gives us the story of this spiritual battle. It started when Satan (Lucifer) was kicked out of heaven because of his pride. Desiring to conquer the throne of God, this battle still continues today. Therefore, realizing the enemy's plot of eternal destruction, our next step is established: how to *fight* the battle!

A prepared soldier is one familiar with his weaponry. He has practiced slicing the air with his sword and toiled for hours at the shooting range. The skills of hand-to-hand combat become second nature. A good soldier is one who, (1) identifies the enemy, (2) knows his weaponry and skill level, and (3) is ready to do battle. Ephesians 6:14-18 describes the spiritual armor of God. This verse teaches us to put on the armor each morning with the understanding that we fight not against flesh and blood. According to Ephesians 6:12, our battle is against principalities, the rulers of the darkness, and spiritual wickedness. 2 Corinthians 10:3-6 clarifies that our weapons must be spiritual and not carnal. When we put on the armor of God and proclaim our identity in Him, the enemy trembles. As we stand on the Word of God, which is our spiritual weapon, victories are won, and enemies defeated.

When you don't understand who you are as a Christian, the authority you have as a believer in Christ can be hard to receive. Before this subject of authority is addressed, learning more about the armor that we must put on is essential. So, let's continue into our next lesson concerning the armor of God. But first, listen to what Pappa God has said.

Pappa God's Exhortation

My child, I fought your battles on the cross. Everything that needed to be done was finished when I gave My life for you. I sacrificed My body for your infirmities, healing you and empowering you in My blood. My Word is the footstool that your feet should be planted on, knowing that the battle has been won. But you are here on this earth to walk out all that has been completed in Me. So, stand upon My Word, knowing that this is the weapon I give to you to accomplish what I have already done. *~Pappa God*

1. Do you think that a battle needs to be fought after knowing that Jesus died on the cross conquering all sins, sickness, and all that the enemy uses to kill, steal, and destroy? How and Why?

2. What are some ways that the enemy steals, kills, and destroys? Explain and show scriptures of ways he likes to destroy. Talk about how the enemy is fighting you in character and physical destruction.

3. Is there a scripture that says that the battle is not ours, but God's? Do you know how to fight the battle? Do you know what kind of battle it is that needs to be fought?

4. What weapon would you fight this battle with? And how would you fight with this weapon?

5. In our next chapter, we will discuss the armor of God, but at this moment, do you believe that you are equipped with God's armor, to be able to fight this battle?

6. Do you put this armor on every day?

7. Do you believe that having God's armor on will protect you during the day? Explain how you put the armor on and how it protects you.

8. What did you learn from Pappa God's exhortation?

When entering the military, men and women learn to fight battles in the way the army teaches them. Do you fight your battles the way that God teaches?

Notes of Reflection: _____

Chapter 11

The Armor of God (Part 1)

"Therefore take up the whole armor of God, that
you may be able to withstand in the evil day, and
having done all, to stand. Stand therefore, having
girded your waist with truth, having put on the
breastplate of righteousness..."
(Ephesians 6:13-14 NKJV)

In our last prophetic exhortation from Pappa, He spoke to us concerning how Jesus fought our battles when He went to the cross. Now, it's our responsibility to bring forth the manifestation of the victory in these battles. Jesus did not leave us unequipped with the tools and weapons that were needed. The verse above in Ephesians shares that the whole armor of God is to seize and to withstand evil.

Ephesians 6:14-17 gives us seven pieces of equipment that should be put on daily. When we are suited with the whole armor of God, evil cannot stand against us; therefore, we'll see the victories for which we are fighting. Let's look at the first part of our armor in verse 14: "Stand therefore, having girded your waist with truth, having put on the breastplate of righteousness..." When we gird our waist with truth, we're putting on the belt of Jesus. When the Roman soldiers entered a battle, they always wore their belt of metal around them. A Christian guarded with the truth girded around his waist is protected. Jesus is the way, the truth, and the life and no one can come to the Father except through Jesus. When we know Jesus, truth protects us from the fiery darts of the enemy. The belt of truth holds together the rest of the armor of God. Each piece of the armor will struggle to function if the Spirit of Truth isn't present.

Righteousness means right standing before God. As you wear this breastplate of strength and protection, your heart—like other vital organs—is shielded from the evil darts of the enemy. It was because of the righteousness of God that we have been made righteous. Now, having made Him Lord, He sees us righteous as if we have never sinned. As we continue to live right by choosing to obey and honor Him, the breastplate of His righteousness protects us from the confusing lies of Satan.

Let's continue to put our armor suit on by moving to our next chapter.

Pappa God's Exhortation

My children, I died for your sins and made you righteous in Me. Now, there is no need to fear the battles you must fight. For I have already won them; they're not yours, but Mine. These battles were won in the spirit realm but not the physical. I have equipped you with the armor that will protect and strengthen you. Place your trust in Me; I am your belt of truth that will gird your spirit-man toward victories. *~Pappa God*

1. When you first heard about putting on the armor of God, what did you think it meant?

2. What does it mean to gird your waist with the truth? Explain.

3. What does it mean to have the breastplate of righteousness?

4. How do these two pieces of God's equipment protect you in battle?

5. Do you think these two pieces of armor for battle contradict one another or complement each other? Explain.

6. Read 2 Corinthians 5:21 and explain it.

7. What did you learn from Pappa God's exhortation?

_____

_____

> When Jesus paid the price for our sin on the cross, we
> were made the righteousness of God. Do you believe
> that Jesus died for you? Do you believe that you were
> on the cross with Him?"

Notes of Reflection: _____

Chapter 12

The Armor of God (Part 2)

"...and having shod your feet with the preparation of
the gospel of peace; above all, taking the shield of
faith with which you will be able to quench all the
fiery darts of the wicked one."
(Ephesians 6:15-16 NKJV)

In these next two pieces in the armor of God (listed above), is a connection that people may miss in their reading of this word. Each piece of equipment stands alone but they work together as they are connected to the armor of our warfare. If "faith" is not the platform on which you stand, your confidence in the gospel is weak. Confidence brings the peace of "knowing" that when you have been spiritually equipped, the fears of the wicked have been defeated. You can't have peace unless you have faith. Having the Word within our hearts and knowing that the love of God casts out fears, confusion and doubt won't creep in. The shield of faith is for your protection. Your faith is weak when you have not strengthened your heart in the gospel of the Word. Therefore, turmoil may fill your heart instead of the peace of God.

With that stated, the phrase, "having shod your feet with the preparation of the gospel of peace," actually means that your feet are prepared with strength and confidence, to share with others. As your shoes support your feet, standing on the gospel of truth is peace. Knowing that He is in control, the raging seas of life begin to rest and bring a sense of calm and composure.

When I became a spirit-filled Christian, I experienced God's love and presence around me so strongly that I imagined I walked inside a bubble. That bubble was the shield of His blood surrounding me. I knew that nothing could touch me as long as I remained in that bubble. The bubble was not only His blood, but it was also His love, and His Word embedded deep within my heart. This was my spiritual shield. Isaiah 30:15 (NKJV) tells us, "In quietness and confidence shall be your strength." Today, as I quietly trust in the Word of God, my confidence grows deeper and my shield becomes stronger. Because of the shield of faith, I can trust that my steps have been ordered by the Lord. Therefore, I have peace and a calm spirit within.

Next, let's look at two more areas of equipment, which are necessary to complete our armor suit. But first, let's hear the heart of Pappa.

Pappa God's Exhortation

As I have spoken to you about the different pieces of My suit of armor, know that each one walks in conjunction with the other. As a domino falls in line, these parts will fit together according to their need. Understanding that the importance of each part of the armor of Christ is like a puzzle that depends on each piece to complete it. Faith is the platform where the other pieces of the armor connect. Peace is the glue that holds it all together. My suited warriors then become My ambassadors of My Word. ~*Pappa God*

1. The word *shod* means to shoe. Are the shoes that you wear filled with the gospel of truth? Are they filled with the peace of God?

2. If "no," what do you walk in: a fear, a doubt, insecurity of identity, or maybe, confidence? Many ungodly emotions try to fill our shoes with characteristics that are unlike Christ. Explain. What fills *your* shoes?

3. Do you think truth is peace that brings a calm and assured walk with Jesus? Explain.

4. This shoe should be a perfect fit for you. If not, you will be uncomfortable. Could it be that your relationship with Jesus is a little rocky? If so, why?

5. Do you stand on the platform of faith?

6. How do these two pieces—faith and peace—fit together as God's armor? How do they complement each other. Explain.

7. What did you learn from Pappa God's exhortation?

"When a strong man, fully armed, guards his own palace, his goods are in peace." (Luke 11:21 NKJV)

Notes of Reflection: _____

Chapter 13

The Armor of God (Part 3)

"And take the helmet of salvation, and the sword of
the Spirit, which is the word of God; praying always
with all prayer and supplication in the Spirit."
(Ephesians 6:17-18 NKJV)

To complete our armor suit, the helmet of salvation must "be put on" while taking the sword of the spirit—the Word of God— in our hands. In the previous lesson, we discussed how each of the pieces of equipment work together. So how do they (the helmet of salvation and the sword of the Spirit) complement each other for battle?

Wearing a helmet protects the mind and head from injury in the natural. Spiritually, the enemy tries to confuse you by manipulation, deception, and speaking lies. His tactics will eventually destroy your Godly thoughts if you are not protected. Therefore, having the helmet of salvation on, we are confident, protected, and safe with Jesus as our Lord.

Hebrews 4:12 tells us that the Word of God is sharper than the fiery darts and weapons that the enemy shoots. This verse assures us that the words of God are dangerous when spoken to the enemy. This is the reason God's Word is deep within. He has sealed our hearts with His Word. And with authority, we hold this sword in the palms of our hands, allowing the Holy Spirit to draw from His weapons that have been hidden deep within. Now, with our double-edged sword, we are ready to fight any weapon the enemy sends toward us.

The last tool to discuss as part of our armor suit, is praying. We should always be praying with supplication, with a contrite heart, in the Spirit. Prayer along with peace is the glue of our armor suit that keeps each piece of equipment in tact. The Father knows what we have need of and He hears our request. We demonstrate the dependence we have on Him to be our provider and giant killer, by standing on His promises. Our prayer of faith changes things, and moves the heart of God. Prayer stirs the atmosphere for our heavenly army of angels. While intercessory prayers are sent up to the Father, warring angels are ready for their assignment of spiritual battle.

His protective, spiritual armor should be "put on" daily in our lives, which is an act of clothing ourselves in Christ from the enemy of evil.

Pappa God's Exhortation

I have given to you every weapon within My Word that will cause the enemy to flee from you. My armor is given to you to put on daily. It is to protect you and give you confidence that you are guarded by My love. I have done ALL for you, but it stands useless unless you apply My Word in your heart and by your actions. I hear your heart when you pray with supplication. Don't stop! It is time to put on what I have given to you, and wear the clothing that I have prepared as your armor ~*Pappa God*

1. What does it mean to put on a spiritual helmet? Why would this be listed as part of the armor of God?

2. Is the sword a spiritual or physical weapon that is used in battle? Would you consider the sword to be the main weapon? Give scriptures to show that we should use our sword in our battles.

3. Where in our body can we find the sword? Are their more places that one?

4. From each area of our armor suit, how do we use this spiritual sword? Give scriptures to back each part of this armor suit.

5. What kind of battles do we fight and when do we fight them?

6. How do we clothe ourselves with the armor of God?

7. What does supplication mean? Why do we need to pray with supplication?

8. Philippians 4:6 tells us that we should not be anxious, but in everything by prayer and supplication, with thanksgiving, let our requests be made known to God. How does this scripture complement Ephesians 6:17-18?

9. What did you learn from Pappa God's exhortation?

"The enemy cannot read the mind, but he can put thoughts in your head, and then look for your agreement."
Bill Johnson, Bethel Church

Notes of Reflection: _____

Chapter 14

He Needed to Go this Way

"Therefore, when the Lord knew that the Pharisees had
heard that Jesus made and baptized more disciples
than John (though Jesus Himself did not baptize, but
His disciples), He left Judea and departed again to
Galilee. But He needed to go through Samaria."
(John 4:1-4 NKJV)

Jesus spoke about three events mentioned in the above four
verses:

1) The Lord knew that the Pharisees believed that
Jesus was baptizing and making more disciples.
However, they didn't realize that it was the disciples,
not Jesus.

2) Jesus knew that the disciples were ready to be
launched out in this assignment.

3) Jesus knew that He needed to go through Samaria
for the appointment arranged by God with the woman
at the well.

The Father, the Son, and the Holy Ghost—three in one—are
omnipresent. Jesus, in this era, knew the future events for each
of these points before they occurred. He knew what the
Pharisees were thinking, and He knew that His followers were
ready to step out to make disciples and baptize the hungry

souls. He also knew what the Samaritan woman who came to draw water from Jacob's well, needed. She hungered and thirsted for the springs of living water, although she had no idea what that was. She needed forgiveness for the husbands that she tried to hide. Jesus saw through the guilt, and touched the core of her heart with His Agape Love.

Jesus hears the cries of your heart, and He knows what you need. He sees when you endure loneliness, unworthiness, and feel forgotten. He knows the thirst and hunger you have for true love and relationships when you've encountered hurt and pain. Jesus knows what you need.

The Father will "set us up" in the place where our needs can be met. Years ago, I had slipped away from the Lord, engaging in the ways of the world. And Jesus knew that my heart was tired of the worldly games of sin. Everywhere I went, I ran into Jesus-talking people—Christians of a previous church asking about my life in Christ. Unable to give the answer they were looking for, I tried dodging these Godly traps (that was my name for them). However, already having the truth within, seeing the trap that the enemy planted became a reality for me of what Satan was doing. I wasn't in the right condition nor position to be talking about Christ, but He was speaking to me. As time went on, I saw that Jesus was setting me up. He knew where and when His words would touch my heart. He met me where I was! And when I was ready to say "Yes," His arms stretched out to welcome me home.

Are you like the Samaritan woman, hungry for truth to set you free from a life of lies and sin? Jesus knows where you are. Therefore, when He speaks to you, don't let the enemy steal away your day of salvation and freedom!

Pappa God's Exhortation

As I knew the heart of the Samaritan woman, I also know *your* heart and what you need. If you let Me, I'll fulfill and satisfy your hunger and thirst with the springs of living water. Your well will never run dry as long as you stay connected to the Vine of life, where your destiny awaits you. *~Pappa God*

1. Jesus, knowing all things, knew He needed to go a certain way on His journey. Have you ever felt like you needed to go in a particular direction other than what your flesh or the voice of others was saying? Was the reason plain to see or was another explanation from the Father given to you as to why? Explain.

2. When Jesus arrived at the area, did He bombard the woman with questions, accusations, or a manipulative, accusing spirit?

3. What kind of character did Jesus show to the women? Do you think He knew that she needed to hear what He had to say with tenderness? Explain.

4. Why didn't the Samaritan women run from this Jew? Did He seem different to her?

5. Was there a hunger inside this women that she didn't know existed? Do you think this was the reason that Jesus had to "go this way?"

6. Was this a "set up" from God? For what was this "set up"?

_____

_____

7. If the Father knows of your needs, does He "set you up" for you to receive them? Do you realize that such a moment is a "set up?"

_____

_____

8. What did you learn from Pappa God's exhortation?

_____

_____

> "If anyone thirsts, let him come to Me and drink. He who believes in Me, as the Scripture has said, out of his heart will flow rivers of living water." (John 7:37b-38 NKJV)

Notes of Reflection: _____

Chapter 15

A Picture of the Church—
Without Spot

"...that He might present her to Himself a glorious
church, not having spot or wrinkle or any such thing,
but that she should be holy and without blemish."
(Ephesians 5:27 NKJV)

Have you ever thought about what Jesus meant by "spot,
wrinkle, and blemish" in the above verse? What are they and
what does this verse mean? Have you ever thought about
whether you have spots, wrinkles, or blemishes? Realizing
these words used in this verse are very closely related to one
another, they stand alone in their purpose. Let's examine each
one and watch how they link together to show us a picture of
the church.

A *spot is* associated with something that is stained, dirty,
or soiled. As I pondered on the verse above and the meaning
of *spots*, my life flashed before me. It was as though I saw
myself in a mirror under a blacklight. A list of worldly sins
appeared. Galatians 5:19 lists them as the sins of the flesh. I
call them "big sins," or those big foxes that spoil the vine. Not
that I was guilty of all, but I saw my areas of fault.

In this list were adultery, fornication, uncleanness, lewdness,
idolatry, sorcery, hatred, contentions, jealousies, outbursts of
wrath, selfish ambitions, dissensions, heresies, envy, murders,
drunkenness, and revelries. Sins of the flesh, like these, expose
themselves to the outside world demonstrating the ways of evil

and unclean spirits. The Word of God says in 1 Corinthians 6:9-10, that the unrighteous, or those who participate in these "ungodly sins/spots," will not inherit the kingdom of God.

When Christ died on the cross for us, our flesh was crucified with Him. We no longer live but it is Christ who lives within. The "old," fleshly sin has passed away and the "new" ways of God are adopted. Jesus took our sins and threw them into the sea of forgetfulness, never to remember them again, leaving us spotless, righteous, and justified—no longer stained, dirty, or soiled.

However, Satan doesn't leave with ease or by the pointed finger. He continues to fight to keep us in bondage, by keeping the old sins alive. Even though forgiveness and freedom are received, the stain of their presence remains. Now, this stain of past sins becomes harder to remove and begins to stink and spoil like rotten fruit.

Spots could mean that total surrender in a sin or sins still straddles the fence. Or those ungodly behaviors could still be hanging around.

Jesus said we are the church, and the church must be without spots. But is this possible when we haven't seen complete surrender and deliverance? It is possible in Him. Jesus sees our heart and knows our struggle in those stubborn areas. He also gave to us His Word that gives the answers we all seek. Deuteronomy 28:1-2 encourages us to obey His commands and His voice, and these blessings will come upon you. But Hebrew 10:26-27 states that if we sin willfully, after knowing the truth, there no longer remains a sacrifice.

Realizing that Jesus has completed His part, we need to do the same. Repentance means to turn away and not engage in that sin any longer. Yes, walking away can be difficult, but Jesus sees our heart of determination to defeat this issue. The

Holy Spirit is always ready to lead and guide us to the verses that will comfort and empower us in the moment.

Let's continue in this series and see what the Father says about the wrinkles in our life. What are they and where do they come from?

Pappa God's Exhortation

My church, My people, will not have spots with the soils and stains of this world. I have removed them when My Son Jesus, died on the cross. I severed the worldly ties that bind you when I washed you white as snow. Now you have become righteous in My eyes; therefore, go and sin no more.

~ *Pappa God*

1. When Jesus said that your sins were washed in His blood and He paid the price for them on the cross, why do you feel it is necessary to keep sinning? Having already discussed this in earlier chapters, why do repetitive actions continue and why are bondages and chains hard to break? Explain.

2. Do you believe that He threw your sins out into the sea of forgetfulness and they are as far as the east is to the west, never to remember them? If He doesn't remember our sins, then why haven't we forgotten them and forgiven ourselves?

3. Past sins create spots that will destroy and stain our life forever, if not removed. The stains and the remembrance of the "old man" can keep us struggling. Looking back over the previous chapters (with their key points), could stains be removed by applying these actions in our life? Explain.

4. Did you surrender them 100 percent, determined not to return to them?

5. Do you believe there is complete freedom in this struggle? If so, where does your answer come from? Explain.

6. What did you learn from Pappa God's exhortation?

Have you shared with others how Jesus has touched your heart, explaining how His love makes you feel protected, warm, and loved? If not, make it a goal to share with someone about his love.

Notes of Reflection: _____

Chapter 16

The Wrinkles Have to Go

*"...that He might present to Himself a glorious church,
not having spot or wrinkle or any such thing..."*
(Ephesians 5:27 NKJV)

In the above scripture, Jesus informs us that He is returning for a church without spot or wrinkle. These two words, *spot* or *wrinkle*, stand together in the scripture, but why? In our previous lesson, we discussed spots. These unclean areas can be leftovers not yet defeated, and will keep us from God's best. When total surrender or death has not taken place, these spots resurrect as thorns in our flesh. These worldly "leftovers" of sin may remain in our life, either by choice, by being unattended to, or the process of their removal may take time. Signs of ungodly characteristics in our mannerisms, the language we use, unclean thoughts, and selfish emotions, mark our identity. An ungodly picture starts to unfold more than the likeness of Christ. These areas in our life are called *wrinkles*.

The Synonym Finder by J.I. Rodale, gives the meaning of the word *wrinkle*, as to fold, crease, crimp, and gather, but how is it used in the scripture above? According to *Dake's Annotated Reference Bible*, the word *wrinkle* in the Greek means *rhutis* and is translated as, "no mark of age." However, the wrinkles on our face show that age has surpassed those youthful years, as gray hair would show the years of wisdom.

When we look at the story of Shadrach, Meshach, and Abednego, and their time in the fiery furnace, their exit was without the smell of smoke or burn marks. Could it have been

93

because of their faith that God was with them in the furnace? Yes! God would not have left them alone.

In the natural, wrinkles can appear by aging and other lifestyle changes, but let's look at the meaning of wrinkles with a different twist. A wrinkle is a fold, crease, crimp or gather, but how in the world can you make these words be spiritual? Well, put your deep thinking caps on, and stay with me during this explanation.

The wrinkles in our life keep us in bondage to sins that will cripple and defeat our destiny in the kingdom. Although we have been washed and forgiven of our sins by the blood of Jesus, doors still remain open, letting us know that we may still be uncommitted to total surrender. We still hang on to habits that hook with their claws of "dependence." Satan continues to feed us with excuses or reasons why the doors can't be shut completely. Here are a few major lies that he speaks: (1) I need it *now*: can't wait! (2) Can't live without it, or (3) One more time won't hurt me. Lies from the enemy with doubts, confusion, and ungodly decisions keep us attached to previous and old thinking. This makes total surrender even harder and allows wrinkles to develop.

So, how do wrinkles fold, crease, crimp, and gather? (1) A *fold* could be the crease when the shirt is not flat, and it overlaps itself. A fold could be the grieving that we give the Holy Spirit in our life. His plans and purposes in our life become camouflaged by hidden sin. Can you see inside a folded piece of paper? No, not until you unfold the paper can you tell what is inside (Ephesians 4:26-31). (2) *Creases* keep a starched shirt from being perfectly smooth. If it has a flaw in it, perfection doesn't exist. (3) A *crimped* hose stops or delays water from flowing through. This can also happen with disobedience. If Christ tells us to stop drinking alcohol completely but we still have that social or bedtime drink, we're in disobedience. This may crimp the style and direction of the Holy Spirit. (4) The last explanation of wrinkles, is *gather*. Satan is the father of lies and confusion. He likes to gather these lies and this confusion into a pile that creates bondage. This bondage creates a spirit of chaos, gathering together to overwhelm us. So, when wrinkles of sin show themselves in our actions and character, the notification button alerts us that more change is needed, and open doors must be shut.

Can you think of some areas in your life that have wrinkles? Do creases need to be smoothed out? Are there folds with things that overlap each other, where you're trying to cover up what you don't want seen? Are there crimped areas that are quenching the Holy Spirit from moving? And finally, is there an overwhelming confusion of questions unsolved (but the answers lie within)? Take a moment to allow the Holy Spirit to search deep in your heart and highlight those areas you cannot see. These wrinkles have to go.

At the end of this scripture in Ephesians, Jesus lets us know the destination point of removing the spots and wrinkles from our life. But first we need to get rid of the blemishes, which we'll discuss in our next lesson.

Pappa God's Exhortation

I Am Who I Say I Am, and My Church, My people will not show spots with the soils and stains of this world. I removed them when My Son, Jesus died on the cross. Therefore, the wrinkles that remain are ironed out when obedience of My Word is rendered. You must be without Spot or Wrinkle. ~*Pappa God*

1. What do you think Jesus means by the word *wrinkles* that is spoken of in Ephesians 5:27? Explain.

2. Are wrinkles connected to spots, which were mentioned in our last chapter? How?

3. How would you explain the Greek meaning of the word *wrinkles* as being, "no mark of age"?

4. Looking at *The Synonym Finder* by J.I. Rodale, and the meaning of the word *wrinkles*, what do you think about the spiritual connotation?

5. Do you have wrinkles in your life that need to be ironed out?

6. Could wrinkles cover up areas in our life that are hidden? Spiritually speaking, how is that possible and what does it look like?

7. Have wrinkles crippled you from receiving all that God has for you? How?

8. What did you learn from Pappa God's exhortation?

A Spiritual Example: When I took a blouse out of the dryer it was full of wrinkles. It either dried too long or not long enough. Therefore, it needed to be ironed. However, this issue could have been resolved had I read the care instructions first. The instructions for this type of material were to dry on a cool setting for ten minutes only. Reading and obeying the instructions could have eliminated these wrinkles. As we read the Word of God, we can avoid the messes that occur in our life, sooner, rather than later.

Notes of Reflection: _____

Chapter 17

No Blemishes

"...that He might present to Himself a glorious
church, not having spot or wrinkle or any such thing,
but that she should be holy and without blemish."
(Ephesians 5:27 NKJV)

As we start to finalize this verse with more clarity toward what kind of church Jesus is returning for, one last word needs to be discussed: *blemishes.*

Spots (sin) can take root in more than one place in our soul. Both spots and wrinkles appear on the outer surface, and are closely related. However, the word *blemish* in a spiritual and carnal way, represents scars that root within. Let's look at its meaning with an example. A blemish, according to Google (by Oxford Languages), is a small flaw which spoils the appearance of something. For example, a young seventeen-year-old boy suffers with teenage acne. Red filled bumps with pus inside appear on his face. When this yellowish infected liquid is removed from the bump, healing begins. However, if treated incorrectly, the sign of a blemish or scar could remain on his face. This process is the last step when spots and wrinkles are healing. Why? The scar or the outward flaw (the blemish) has now wounded his soul. Being embarrassed or insecure with his appearance, deeper wounds may occur within the soul.

Sins can still remain as blemishes in our life. When we are unable to finish the healing process because of excuses and embarrassment, the enemy has interrupted God's plan toward victory. This leaves the process unfinished with those unwanted scars. Spots (sin) are removed, and wrinkles have been ironed out, but the blemishes remain. Surface blemishes have deepened beneath the skin, and the roots must be removed for total freedom to occur. If these scars/blemishes have not been uprooted, the flesh continues to battle with issues that may cripple and cause destruction.

Christ sees and knows our struggle with these blemishes that remain deep within our soul. But we may not realize that an unattended blemish creates havoc in our life. When He gives us an opportunity to go deeper in our soul for cleansing, it's our responsibility to act upon His request.

In the book of Malachi 1:14, the explanation of why He returns for a church without blemishes, is given to us (NKJV): "But cursed be the deceiver who has in his flock a male, and takes a vow, but sacrifices to the Lord what is blemished—for I am a great King, says the Lord of hosts, and My name is to be feared among the nations."

This Old Testament verse speaks of the curse that is upon us when we bring sacrifices to Him that are blemished. Not surrendering these areas to Jesus, the sin that remains continues to be unclean and a curse. Satan will continue to deepen this soul wound until it is renounced and cut away from our life. Because Christ lives within, we are no longer cursed. We are forgiven, redeemed, renewed, revived, and reborn.

Let me share another example: imagine a large tree in the forest. When you examine it, you notice that knots are on the trunk leaving an unsmooth but rugged look. However, in some areas the bark has been pulled away, exposing the unclothed tree. Its true beauty has been camouflaged because of the flaws on it. After this tree is cut down and sent to the timber yards to be shaved and shaped for lumber, we then see its true beauty appear.

This is what blemishes—or the remaining sins—appear like in our life. When we allow Jesus to shave and peel away, and we die to those old sins, our beauty shines through. Our true identity starts to appear, and God's creative vessels of holiness blossom.

Now, in our next lesson, let's discuss the holiness that Jesus seeks in us.

Pappa God's Exhortation

I have allowed the spots, wrinkles, and blemishes to appear in your life for a reason. Realizing that your life is not perfect, you now have a need for a Savior to restore your true identity. My creation was pure and without the deformities of this world; however, you were given a choice and your choice was not Me. My Son will return for My church which will not be spoiled nor stained with the presence of sin. My church, My people, will be holy.
~*Pappa God*

1. What does the word *blemish* mean, according to Google (by Oxford Languages), and describe how the church has these blemishes? Is the church doing anything about it?

2. Are blemishes the results of sin, brokenness, and wounds in our life? What does that look like?

3. An old saying is: "If you cannot see your reflection in a pot of gold that is being melted, then impurities still remain." How do you compare this with seeing your picture in the mirror instead of the one who created you? What are these impurities called?

4. Can blemishes be harmful to one's self esteem? How?

5. Have you had a sin that has scarred you with blemishes that destroyed your identity through damaged emotions? Has it damaged your relationships with others? Explain.

6. What does the Bible say about how you clean and remove these blemishes? Explain.

7. What did you learn from Pappa God's exhortation?

"but the precious blood of Christ—who like a spotless, unblemished lamb was scarified for us." (1 Peter 1:19 TPT)

Notes of Reflection: _____

Chapter 18

To Be Holy

"...that He might present to Himself a glorious
church, not having spot or wrinkle or any such thing,
but that she should be holy and without blemish."
(Ephesians 5:27 NKJV)

Having discussed spots, wrinkles, and blemishes previously, the above verse informs us that these marks of sin will not enter into heaven—only a church that is holy. So, what does this holy church look like in the eyes of God?

In Hebrew, the definition of "holy" means, to be "set apart" or to be rooted in the ways of God. In Genesis 17:1, God tells Abraham to walk before Him and be blameless. Blameless is another word for innocent or having no wrong in your life. In 2 Samuel 22:21-25, Samuel was rewarded because of his clean hands and being blameless before the Lord. Appearing before the Lord blameless, is holy. All spots and wrinkles have been removed, and the blemishes that have scarred are gone. Let's look at a few Biblical verses that will help us understand the meaning of holiness in the eyes of God.

God spoke of being "set apart" in Leviticus 20:26 (NKJV): "And you shall be holy to Me, for I the Lord am holy, and have separated you from the peoples, that you should be Mine." From the very beginning, God separated us from the world by saying that we are His. 1 Peter 1:15-16 (NKJV) says, "but as He who called you is holy, you also be holy in all your conduct, because it is written, 'Be holy, for I am holy.'" A call to be holy is from the one who created us, in His image. So, to be holy like

Him is not a strange idea from the outer limits of God. It is His purpose for those whom He has called and chosen. Jesus was a sinless man, making Him holy (John 8:46)! If we have been created in His image, then we are to be holy as He is.

One of the ways to become holy is by being obedient to His Word. Obedience is the number one key that will cause us to become like Him. Research these verses about holiness:

- Walk in His ways (Hosea 14:9)
- Hate evil, love good (Amos 5:15)
- Lips purified (Zephaniah 3:9)
- A key to holiness (Romans 12:1-2)
- An attitude of mind and lifestyle (Philippians 4:8-9)

These are just a few verses of what the Word has to say.

James 4:4 says that we are adulterers when a friendship with the world has occurred. This becomes enmity with Him (one who makes himself an enemy of God). This is not the separation that God proposed. To "be separated" in Him, is to become holy.

Ephesians 5:1 also reminds us that we should be imitators of God as dear children. Therefore, as we learn to walk like Him, our talk, our actions, and our heart begins to change. We begin to be more heavenly minded, sacred, set apart from the world while we seek His miracles and mysteries. These changes start to happen because we have dedicated and devoted our lives to become like Him.

Spots, wrinkles, and blemishes will cease when God's people become holy as He is holy. As we begin to seek the One True God, spots, wrinkles, and blemishes are removed. Becoming holy as He is holy is a daily walk and sacrifice of dying to the flesh. Listen to the words of Pappa.

Pappa God's Exhortation

As you seek holiness as I am holy, sin will not reign in your life, your thoughts, or your actions. Your ways will become like Mine when your heart seeks after goodness. As darkness cannot stand in the midst of light, neither can evil and blemishes of sin, in holiness. My kingdom is holy. Therefore, only holiness will be found in My Kingdom. *~Pappa God*

1. What does the word *holy* mean in the eyes of God or in the Hebrew?

2. How can you be holy in a world of evil? Explain. Does the Bible give us scripture to follow and walk in to become holy?

3. Can you be holy and have spots, wrinkles, and blemishes? Explain.

4. In your own words explain Ephesians 5:27.

5. With scripture, list some of the ways that you can start to become holy in your life and in general for the body of Christ.

6. How does your heart and obedience play a role in becoming holy? Explain.

7. What did you learn from Pappa God's exhortation?

_____

_____

| "And in love he chose us before he laid the foundation of the universe! Because of his great love, he ordained us, so that we would be seen as holy in his eyes with an unstained innocence." (Ephesians 1:4 TPT) |

Notes of Reflection: _____

Chapter 19

Spirit, Soul, and Body— The Spirit

"Then the dust will return to the earth as it was,
and the spirit will return to God who gave it."
(Ecclesiastes 12:7 NKJV)

After God created the heavens and the earth, He created man, and breathed life into his nostrils. Before Eve ate of the forbidden tree, man's spirit, in the eyes of God, was perfect. However, sin entered Eve's heart when she disobeyed the Father.

Before the physical body was developed in the womb, God created our spirit with the identity of who we are in Him. But, because of sin, this identity—our spirit, soul, and body—has become corrupted, unholy, and unclean, and must be born again.

Look at what Jesus spoke to Nicodemus in John 3:4-7 (NKJV) when he questioned how one could be born again: "...unless one is born of water and the Spirit, he cannot enter the kingdom of God. That which is born of the flesh is flesh, and that which is born of the Spirit is spirit. Do not marvel that I said to you, 'You must be born again.'" Jesus informed Nicodemus that his spirit needed to be reborn.

As we break this verse down, we see that there is a difference in the two baptisms: water, and spirit. Let's take a quick look.

When the old carnal man has died and we are water baptized (immersed, not sprinkled), he rises up out of the water as a new man in Christ. Why? The water is symbolic of your sins cleansed and washed away. This is a baptism of repentance. Mark 1:4-5 (NKJV) states, "John came baptizing in the wilderness and preaching a baptism of repentance for the remission of sins. Then all the land of Judea, and those from Jerusalem, went out to him and were all baptized by him in the Jordan River, confessing their sins."

After John baptized with water, he spoke of one whose sandals he was not worthy to loose. This was Jesus, the Lamb of God who takes away the sins of the world! When Jesus appeared, John saw the Spirit descending from heaven like a dove and rested upon Him (John 1:26-34). It was then that John heard these words, "'Upon whom you see the Spirit descending, and remaining on Him, this is He who baptizes with the Holy Spirit'" (John 1:33b NKJV). John testified that this is the Son of God.

Now that we understand that the Father has sent the Son to wash away our sins, our spirit has been reborn and eternal salvation has come. However, our soul is still lost and stands in disagreement with our newborn spirit. Our soul, which is our mind, will, and emotions, must die to the ways of the flesh—they are still lost. In our next lesson, we will start to understand why and how the soul does not agree with our newborn Spirit.

If your spirit has never been reborn into the kingdom of God, here are the five steps to receive eternal life: (1) Ask Jesus to forgive you of your sins, by repentance and water baptism, (2) Ask Him to become your Lord and Savior, (3) Believe that Jesus died on the cross and has risen from the grave, (4) Seek the baptism in water and His Holy Spirit, and (5) Get involved in a Spirit-filled, believing church.

Pappa God's Exhortation

Only that which is of My Spirit shall enter the kingdom of God; therefore, return to Me. Wash yourselves in My Word and be filled with My Holy Spirit, so you will become My vessels of honor. Flesh and bone shall "be left behind," but the spirit lives forever. Heed the words of My Son, that you must be born again. *~Pappa God*

1. Would you be confused if you heard the phrase "Ye must be born again" like Nicodemus? What would your feelings be?

2. Explain how one can be reborn in water and reborn in the spirit? What happens in this transformation?

3. Why does the Spirit baptism mean more to God than the water baptism? Explain.

4. When God breathed life into man's nostrils, was that from His Spirit?

5. Is there a difference between receiving the Spirit of God when life was blown into your lungs, and the Pentecostal experience in Acts 2? Explain.

6. Do you need both encounters? Why? Explain.

7. Is there a difference between the spirit and the flesh? Explain this difference.

8. What did you learn from Pappa God's exhortation?

"'Watch and pray, lest you enter into temptation. The spirit indeed is willing, but the flesh is weak.'"
(Mark 14:38 NKJV)

Notes of Reflection: _____

Chapter 20

Spirit, Soul, and Body— The Soul

"Now may the God of peace Himself sanctify you through and through [that is, separate you from profane and vulgar things, make you pure and whole and undamaged—consecrated to Him—set apart for His purpose]; and may your spirit and soul and body be kept complete and [be found] blameless at the coming of our Lord Jesus."
(1 Thessalonians 5:23 AMP)

God created man as a three-part being. Man has a spirit, which is God's. Man has a soul that is his. And man has a body as an outer covering. The soul also has three-parts—the mind, will, and emotions—which make up the character of the flesh.

Before we look at each of these parts, we must realize that unlike the Spirit, the soul cannot be saved: it must be changed. As the Word teaches us about our mind, will, and emotions, we see the difference between the flesh and the spirit.

As the above scripture tells us, our soul must be pure, sound, complete, and found blameless when Jesus returns. As individual parts, the mind, will, and emotions must be in accordance. In chapter eighteen, "To Be Holy," several verses were mentioned pertaining to becoming "holy," blameless in sin, and dying to the soulish, unholy character.

God breathed life into the nostrils of man, and the soul sustains the existence of life by being spiritually and physically healthy. Therefore, each part of the soul must receive the change needed to become sanctified and consecrated before God.

As the soul functions within as a fleshly compartment of the body, it disagrees with the new spiritual life. Now, the reborn spirit battles old sinful ways of the flesh that come from the mind, will, and emotions. Change must take place within the soul for the body to be able to perform the assignments of the Spirit of the Lord.

In the next lesson, let's look at the mind of the flesh, and how it must be renewed. Proverbs 19:16 (NKJV) says, "He who keeps the commandment keeps his soul, but he who is careless of his ways will die."

Pappa God's Exhortation

In the beginning of time, I breathed life into your nostrils. And after I sent My son to die on the cross for your sins, My Holy Spirit came upon the earth to walk with you daily. He has filled you with My Spirit to complete you with My presence. But, in order for My Spirit to move in the earth, the mind, will, and emotions of the soul must agree to My ways. As light and darkness do not mix, neither does My Spirit agree with the ways of the world. Change is needed for the soul to comprehend My ways; therefore, death to the flesh and carnal ways must take place. *~Pappa God*

1. If you live in this world, how do you separate your soul from it? Explain using scripture.

2. What does the soul consist of in the body?

3. Are these parts or areas saved? How would you know if these soul compartments are saved or line up with the spirit? Explain.

4. If your spirit was saved but the soul is still connected to the ways of the world, do you think it would be hard to become Christ-like? Explain using scripture.

5. What does this verse from Proverbs, mean: "There is a way which seemeth right unto a man, but the end thereof are the ways of death" (Proverbs 14:12 KJV)?

6. Is the soul involved in Proverbs 14:12? In what way?

7. What did you learn from Pappa God's exhortation?

| All that comforts the flesh (soul), weakens the spirit. |

Notes of Reflection: _____

Chapter 21

The Mind

"For to be carnally minded is death, but to be
spiritually minded is life and peace."
(Romans 8:6 NKJV)

As we learned in our last lesson, the soul must be changed. The *mind*, which is of the soulish realm, is considered to be the playground or the battlefield of the enemy. Realizing that a playground can be dangerous, rules for the protection of children are necessary. Unwanted intruders can attack and cause harm. The mind also must be protected and guarded by the Word of God. If not, Satan will steal, kill, and destroy.

The above verse from Romans lets us know that to be carnally minded is death. But what does that mean? Romans 8:5 (NKJV) says: "For those who live according to the flesh set their minds on the things of the flesh, but those who live according to the Spirit, the things of the Spirit."

Here is an example: if I told you that I was going to the bar tonight and had planned on drinking and doing whatever, my *mind* is not on Jesus, but on pleasing my flesh. This is the carnally minded that is headed for spiritual death. If my mind thought about the things of the Spirit of God, I would think on objects that were pure, clean, and acceptable unto Him or on the things above, and not on things of this earth. (See Philippians 4:8 and Colossians 3:2).

Isaiah 55:8-9 says that God's ways and thoughts are not like ours. The mind becomes the battlefield or playground for the enemy to attack, when our thoughts are not embracing the ways of Christ. Therefore, when we allow the flesh to become dominant in our life, we cannot please God (Romans 8:8). Although we have the mind of Christ (1 Corinthians 2:16), because of sin, the mind must be renewed and changed. This transformation proves God's love, and that His character can live within us. It shows others that these changes have taken place within, and *their* mind can also be renewed (Romans 12:2).

So how do we renew our mind to please God and not the flesh? The Bible is full of scriptures that help us in our daily walk to become like Christ. I believe this verse in Proverbs 23:7 (NKJV) establishes our first step after salvation: "For as he thinks in his heart, so is he." The mind thinks about what is in the heart. If your heart has not repented, then your flesh is still interacting with sin. Keeping your mind on sinful things will bring spiritual death. If you have allowed Jesus in your heart, and walked away from the old, then you'll desire to think about clean and pure things. Therefore, your mind has been renewed or is in the process. An urge to get closer to God will dominate your thoughts. When our heart has been saved and cleansed, our thoughts, dreams, and visions will be transformed also.

Pappa God's Exhortation

I see your deeds and they are good, but your mind is far from Me. Seeking to please the self and the ways of the world is carnal and is not pleasing to Me. I have given you My mind; carnal thoughts and ways are not acceptable in My Kingdom. You must be spiritually-minded—opposed to the fleshly ways of the world, when entering the gates of heaven. As you seek My Word, the Holy Spirit will guide you into a renewed mind. *~Pappa God*

1. How would you describe living in the flesh compared to living holy for Christ? Explain.

2. Do you walk more in the Spirit or the flesh? Can you explain how and why?

3. What can you change to be more holy in the eyes of God? Do you truly desire to be holy like He is Holy?

4. Is your mind the playground where Satan likes to cause confusion or speak lies? What are you doing about it?

5. What does your heart want more of than anything in life?

6. The Word says that as a man thinks, so is he. If your mind is on the things of the world, will you start acting like it? What

happens if you keep your mind on the Word of God?

_____

_____

7. Do you keep your mind on the things above or on the things of the earth?

_____

_____

8. Is this statement true or false: "whatever I think about I will eventually start to believe, and then start to walk in it"? Explain your answer.

_____

_____

9. What did you learn from Pappa God's exhortation?

_____

_____

> I will not allow Satan to deceive me in my mind
> by words that are powerless!
> *Shelia Humphries*

Notes of Reflection: _____

Chapter 22

Emotions

"So above all, guard the affections of your heart,
for they affect all that you are. Pay attention to the
welfare of your innermost being, for from there
flows the wellspring of life."
(Proverbs 4:23 TPT)

The Passion Translation clarifies this verse in a beautiful way. Guarding your affections is a protected covering over your *emotions*. This is a big responsibility that God has placed within us. Having this responsibility to protect these emotions can be difficult if not equipped with the correct model to guide you. Jesus is and should be our spiritual model. As we look at His life, we see that He was moved by His affections, not His emotions within His heart. Having a heart of love, His emotions developed His character that He walked in daily.

So how do the emotions that we carry within, develop God's character? The only way that this question can be answered is by studying our model: Jesus. In Galatians 5:22 (NKJV), we see His character, or His emotions. "But the fruit of the Spirit is love, joy, peace, longsuffering, kindness, goodness, faithfulness, gentleness and self-control." He was love because He loved. He was joy because He brought life. He was faithful because He is a man who cannot lie. He was peaceful because He knew who He was and to whom He belonged. Seeing that His character developed because of His love for His Father, He related to people with emotions that spoke from His heart.

God created man in His likeness; the characteristics from the fruit of His Spirit dwell within but are manifested by the affections of our heart. When we have a heart like Him, we desire to love. When we have received life in Christ, we become joyful and happy. Knowing that He was faithful to deliver us from sin, we know that we can always depend on Him. And though our spirit may have been saved from sin, our fleshly emotions must accommodate our new spirit-man in the agreement of transformation.

Having a wounded soul can destroy the development of looking like our model, Jesus. These emotions become ungodly and show their ugly face at times, because of hurt, pain, trauma, or the resemblance of worldly characteristics instead of Jesus. The little foxes do spoil the vine. Reflecting upon the WWJD bracelet (what would Jesus do?) allows us to see the fruit of His Spirit in action. The affection of His heart and His emotions proclaim the meaning of His name: Love. In the middle of an emotional moment, do we ask what Jesus would do in the situation? The desire to respond in a Godly way does not always happen. Sin may still have a stronghold on our emotions, where deliverance or other methods of healing are needed.

If the affections of your heart are like His, then the character of your emotions will reflect the nature of Jesus.

Pappa God's Exhortation

I have placed Godly characteristics within your emotions. When you allow Me to heal your heart from worldly ways, transformation can take place. Until then, these emotions become ungodly when they continue to live as flesh. The first part of salvation is death to the flesh. A seed cannot grow unless it dies first. So, in order to follow in the footsteps of My son, Jesus, the emotions of the soul have to die. His character is the fruit of My Spirit, which bellows out of His heart. Mimic His emotions, and you'll be fine.
~*Pappa God*

1. Are the affections of your heart the same as your emotions, or do emotions affect your heart?

2. Is the fruit of the Spirit a reflection of the character of Jesus?

3. Do you have the same fruit of Christ? Is your fruit spiritual instead of carnal? Explain. If not, what must you do to change it?

4. How do we become Christ-like or imitators of Him? Explain.

5. Managing your emotions can be difficult at times. What is the process that is needed to continue in order for manifested victories to occur? Explain.

6. What did you learn from Pappa God's exhortation?

Gifts can't take you where your character can.

Notes of Reflection: _____

Chapter 23

The Will

"Not everyone who says to Me, 'Lord, Lord,' shall
enter the kingdom of heaven, but he who does the
will of My Father in heaven."
(Matthew 7:21 NKJV)

In Deuteronomy 1:31 (NIV), Moses encouraged his followers when they were in the wilderness, with this statement: "the Lord your God carried you." God set an example to the Israelites by carrying them before the Christ had come. Now, after the birth and resurrection of Jesus, the opportunity awaits each soul to walk with Him. As we walk with Him, only one set of footprints is visible in the sand, because He is carrying us. When there are two sets of footprints, we have decided to walk on our own. This allegory of "Footprints in the Sand," presents another thought besides our Lord carrying us; it is a notable example of the "will."

Before I accepted Jesus as Lord, no one controlled my life except me. It was my *will* that made the decision to go, what to eat, and what kind of recreational play time I desired to engage in. Self-will led my daily walk. But when Jesus became Lord, my life became His and He began to carry me.

This scripture in Matthew 7:21 tells us that a majority of people believe they will be entering the gates of Heaven by just calling Him, "Lord, Lord." Saying "Yes" to His calling is the first step to eternal life, but those who do the *will* of the Father will enter the kingdom. Aligning our desires with His will is the key. This is when He carries us.

As we have been learning about spirit and soul, the *will* is the key point to renewing the mind and dying to the old emotions and characteristics. Self-will—or the flesh—is a form of pride and walks on the outside of the feet of God. You are living your life, your way. Walking in God's will is when we have allowed Jesus to carry us, or we've stepped upon His feet, and our desire is to walk in His ways. Dying to the flesh or self-will is a process of surrendering our will to His. Yielding our ways to His is a learned behavior of the will that requires daily exercise.

"Teach me to do Your will, for You are my God; Your Spirit is good. Lead me in the land of uprightness" (Psalm 143:10 NKJV).

Yielding our will is a choice. Dying to the old man is a choice. Humbling ourselves is a choice. Total surrender and commitment is a choice. God gave to us the freedom of choice. However, He gave to us the answer in Deuteronomy 30:19: choose life.

Obedience in the *will* of the Father is life. Therefore, He calls us to identity with Him, by walking in His will.

The last of our mini-series of *Spirit, Soul and Body* is the *body*. In this final lesson, we will start to see the importance of taking care of the spiritual and physical body.

Pappa God's Exhortation

I have placed My Word at your fingertips with instructions to follow. Creating you in My image was no mistake and My instructions to be an imitator of Me stand correct. So why do you think that walking through the gates of heaven is so easy? You must be a doer of My Will, not yours. Flesh cannot enter in, only that which is Spirit and does the Will of the Father. Therefore, stand on My feet by dying to your will and let Me carry you. *~Pappa God*

1. What is Jesus talking about in Matthew 7:21 when He mentions His Father's will?

2. If His will is to be done, what does His will entail and how should we make this change?

3. What is the difference between my will and His?

4. What does the poem "Two feet in the Sand" mean?

5. Did you stand on your father's feet and dance with him? What did that feel like to you, emotionally? Do you feel like that when you stand on the feet of God?

6. How does He carry *us*? How does He carry *you*? Explain.

7. An attempt to walk in His will and mine at the same time is called being double-minded. What does God's Word say about being double-minded?

8. What did you learn from Pappa God's exhortation?

> "And do not be conformed to this world: but be ye transformed by the renewing of your mind, that ye may prove what is that good, and acceptable, and perfect, will of God." (Romans 12:2 KJV)

Notes of Reflection: _____

Chapter 24

Spirit, Soul, and Body—
The Body

"For you were bought at a price; therefore glorify God
in your body and in your spirit, which are God's."
(1 Corinthians 6:20 NKJV)

In our past studies, we learned that the spirit and soul are
created to function on their own. In order for each to operate
accurately, they need a place of residence. God created the
body as the tent, outer shell, or container that houses your
spirit and soul.

The body cannot function by itself; it depends on the spirit
and the soul to bring life and instruction to it. When we receive
our new birth in Christ, the spirit is reborn. However, the soul
needs to be crucified of worldly thoughts, fleshly emotions,
and a self-will of pride. The body must agree to the spirit and
soul to avoid an imbalance of spiritual ways. The only way for
this agreement to happen, is when the body has also been
crucified to the flesh or carnal ways of the world.

The verse above in 1 Corinthians tells us that we have a
responsibility to our body. Although Jesus bought us with a
great price through His death on the cross, it's our part to
glorify God in our body. But how is this done?

When I accepted Jesus as Lord, He became a part of my
daily routine in life. My body became the temple of where the
Holy Spirit resides, and the vehicle to share His Word (see 1
Corinthians 3:16). It is my responsibility to make sure that I

am eating correctly as well as getting enough sleep and water to keep the bodily organs functioning normally. It is also my responsibility to keep my spiritual walk strong with the armor of God: glorifying Him through praise and worship, the reading of His Word, and fellowship with Him.

The spirit, soul, and body must be in union with one another. If this union does not occur, an internal war between flesh and spirit can bring defeat. Scripture tells us that bad company corrupts good morals (1 Corinthians 15:33). Applying this concept to our spirit, soul, and body develops a stable understanding for a spiritual walk.

God created man with this spiritual design, for a divine purpose. That purpose is to glorify Him and bring forth His Word to a lost and dying world. We are His vessels to utilize His Kingdom purpose here on earth. If the spirit, soul, and body have not been reborn into the likeness of Him, self-will will attempt Kingdom purposes and fail.

When the soul is out of alignment with the newborn spirit, the body is also. The body as well as the soul must adhere to the changes of the heart. If each is out of balance, our spiritual walk will not perform as it should. The body is the carrier of the new ways of the spirit and the soul that has been transformed into a likeness of Christ.

Pappa God's Exhortation

I have wonderfully designed the human anatomy to where your spirit, soul, and body work together. When the physical and spiritual parts woven together is the tapestry, this three-cord strand is not easily broken. However, sin can break through this bond if the door is open. It's critical that the spirit be reborn, and the flesh is crucified. Your body is My temple, where I reside, so glorify Me in your body. Tending to both the body and spirit and providing what they need is necessary. ~*Pappa God*

1. Spiritually and physically speaking, describe what the "body" is.

2. How does Jesus expect us to take care of our bodies, especially if our bodies are the temple of where the Holy Spirit resides. Explain.

3. Does the body need to be in alignment with the spirit and soul in order to operate successfully? How? Explain.

4. Have we corrupted our bodies from the original creation? How? Explain.

5. What did you learn from Pappa God's exhortation?

What's next is NOW! God is going to give you NOW.
Our job is THANK YOU. His job is NEXT!
Bill Johnson, Bethel Church

Notes of Reflection: _____

Chapter 25

Three Bullets that Can Lead to Death

"No weapon formed against you shall prosper, and
every tongue which rises against you in judgment
you shall condemn."
(Isaiah 54:17 NKJV)

When Lucifer, the fallen angel from Heaven, was kicked out by God, he wasted no time in forming his reputation on Earth. His name changed to Satan, which unpleasantly sounds evil and wicked. As soon as God completed His creation of man, Satan attacked. Adam, formed from the dust of the earth, and Eve, created from the rib of Adam, were perfect in the eyes of God. But Satan had a plan to destroy what God had created for humanity.

Being a schemer, his tricks of manipulation, deception, confusion, and lies plunder through the souls of God's people. His weapon of warfare was three bullets that targeted the heart for death. He was out to kill, steal, and destroy. These bullets found in Genesis 3:1-6 are used by the enemy to sabotage our life. However, they have prepared and equipped us for the days ahead.

This cunning serpent in Genesis 3:1 (NKJV) appeared to Eve with his *first* bullet being a **question**: "Has God indeed said, 'You shall not eat of every tree of the garden?'" Satan started his conversation with Eve by confusing her with this question so she would doubt the words of God. He then moved into his *second* bullet which was to **refute** the word that God had spoken. In verse 4, God told Eve what would happen if she ate from the forbidden tree in the garden; nor was she to touch it, lest she die. But Satan refuted this word by trying to prove or convince her that she would not die. "Then the serpent said to the woman, "You will not surely die." Now, Satan pulls the trigger to his *third* bullet that would **reinterpret** this word to mean something else. In verse 5, Satan says to Eve, "For God knows that in the day that you eat of it your eyes will be opened, and you will be like God, knowing good and evil." Satan reinterpreted the meaning of why she should not eat of the forbidden tree in the garden.

Today, Satan uses these same three bullets to manipulate and deceive us from God's best in our life. Train yourself to listen for the question, the refute, and the reinterpretation from the voice of Satan. Rebuke him and stand on the Word of God that is truth. Know that in Isaiah 54:17, we are told that no weapon that Satan uses against us shall prosper. Encourage yourself by knowing that God is greater than he who is in the world. Then, Satan cannot steal the truth as you stand on and believe God's Word.

Pappa God's Exhortation

In the beginning of creation, I allowed you to see the bullets of corruption that the enemy would use in your life. And in the development of My Word indoctrinated on this earth, I gave each the choice to use My sword as your weapon. No weapon of the enemy will prosper unless you allow it. Stop, listen, and be alerted to the schemes and tools of Satan. They are not Mine! ~*Pappa God*

1. What are the three bullets Satan used to attack Eve? Have you seen them in your life?

2. Take the time to explain each bullet and how it has operated in your life. How have they been different?

3. Can you look back (before you received Christ in your life) and see the order of these bullets that led you astray? Explain.

4. Since Christ has saved you, have you been more aware of these bullets that come again to steal, kill, and destroy you? Can you see them in the lives of others? Can you see them in this world?

5. How have you stopped these bullets from being successful in their kill? Give scriptures and explain.

6. What did you learn from Pappa God's exhortation?

_____

_____

> "Behold, I give you the authority to trample on serpents and scorpions, and over all the power of the enemy, and nothing shall by any means hurt you." (Luke 10:19 NKJV)

Notes of Reflection: _____

Chapter 26

Brilliant Light

"For God, who said, 'Let brilliant light shine out of
darkness,' is the one who has cascaded his light
into us—the brilliant dawning light of the glorious
knowledge of God as we gaze into the face of
Jesus Christ."
(2 Corinthians 4:6 TPT)

"**T**his Little Light of Mine" was a spiritual song believed
to have been written for the enslaved African Americans
before the emancipation. In 1925, the lyrics appeared in a
poetry book by Edward G. Ivins, and were picked up by the
Methodist church and sang as a folk song. Whether or not the
song was sung by diverse groups, the lyrics remained the same.
The mainstream religious groups coupled this song with
Matthew 5:14-16: "You are the light of the world . . . Let your
light so shine before men" (NKJV).

Although the biblical verse reads, "You are the light of the
world," the word *little* was never used in Matthew or in
2 Corinthians. In The Passion Translation, 2 Corinthians 4:6
reads, "Let brilliant light shine out of the darkness" while the
New King James Version uses the word *commanded*: "For it is
the God who commanded light to shine out of the darkness . . ."

As Christians, we have a responsibility, and that is to *shine*,
showing the brilliant light of Christ that is within us! We are
not to hide our joy under a bushel; we are commanded to shine
in the darkness. As a Christian, I believe that we should stand
out in a crowd, making a statement in God's love—showing off

with a brilliant glow that is shining upon our face. As the verse above in 2 Corinthians explains, His light has cascaded into us as a brilliant, dawning light.

In dark places, light always exposes what is not seen. Those who hide in dark and evil places try to prevent their lives from being exposed. The consciousness of sin has been seared, leaving an attitude of not caring; and a sense of wanting to stay "unseen" remains. Yet, God always places His children in the midst of darkness, to shine. Not only does this expose sin, but showing a glow of happiness, peacefulness, and a Godly love, reflects the presence of God. The Word says in Psalm 34:8, "Oh, taste and see that the Lord is good" (NKJV). When a statement of God's goodness has been seen and demonstrated, hearts begin to hunger for what is not within.

The "little light" can easily be put under the bushel and snuffed out. But a brilliant light of Christ shows that you have tasted and seen of His goodness. Now there is a desire to show His love to everyone, and everywhere—that darkness can never prevail. Greater is He who is in you, than the darkness that surrounds.

If Christ lives within your heart as Lord and Savior, don't allow the enemy to steal away your happiness, your peacefulness, and His love. Stand strong on what you know is true by what you've experienced. And show others, by letting your light shine brilliantly for Jesus. This is His commandment.

Pappa God's Exhortation

My children, You are My purpose in the earth; therefore, let Me be your purpose, to shine My light through you, where I expose what is not Mine. My brilliant light leads the way upon the pathway to eternal life for those who know not of My love. As My son, Jesus, needed a place to lay His head, I need My children to allow Me to shine My light brilliantly in these dark days. I command this of you, My child. The days are numbered of when My Son, Jesus, returns for His bride. My heart is for *all* to see My light for eternal salvation. *~Pappa God*

1. In your own words, how would you explain the verses in Matthew 5:14-16 and 2 Corinthians 4:6?

2. In what way or ways do non-Christians see Christ in a person?

3. Do you think that this is one of the ways that God commands His children to walk?

4. Why be a light? What does that really do? Did you see the light of Christ in Christians' lives when you were unsaved? Explain.

5. Is being a light an expectation that Christ has for His children?

6. Explain Psalm 34:8.

_____

_____

7. What did you learn from Pappa God's exhortation?

_____

_____

> "Remember therefore from where you have fallen; repent and do the first works, or else I will come to you quickly and remove your lampstand from its place—unless you repent." (Revelation 2:5 NKJV)

Notes of Reflection: _____

Chapter 27

I'm God's Masterpiece

"I will Praise You, for I am fearfully and wonderfully
made; Marvelous are Your works, and that my
soul knows very well."
(Psalm 139:14 NKJV)

You are God's Masterpiece! And you have a purpose on this earth! Yes, you! You heard me, *you*! It may seem hard to believe, but you were created in the image of God! God gave you a spirit and breathed life into your lungs. He gave you a soul which is your mind, will, and emotions. And He also gave you a body that covers and protects your inner-being.

The Father told Jeremiah in chapter 1:5 that before you were conceived in your mother's womb, the inward man was formed. He even called you by name. He knows all about you! He even planned your future in Him, knowing of your success (Jeremiah 29:11).

So, God knew us before we were conceived and He praises His creation of humanity. However, His heart is saddened when man's decision is separate from Him. He gave to each an opportunity to choose eternal life when He died on the cross. He proved His love for all by taking our place in death. Sadly, this opportunity has been dismissed and this wise decision of eternal life is thrown by the wayside.

Life was created in secret, and each soul was skillfully made. He saw our substance, yet unformed. He made us with the capability to succeed, with talents, a unique personality, feelings, desires, dreams, and emotions. God's heart created us to be Royal Priests, ministers, His workmanship, rich, holy, a chosen generation, a peculiar people, His own special people, sons and daughters, a friend, a brother, His bride, a Holy Nation, a King, an heir, righteous, the Apple of His eye, and leaders, who are WONDERFULLY AND MARVELOUSLY MADE IN HIS IMAGE! These descriptions express how our Father sees us through His eyes. Here are a few of the verses: 1 Peter 2:9-10; Titus 2:14; Deuteronomy 14:2; Jeremiah 29:11; Ephesians 2:10; Isaiah 61:6; Revelation 1:5-9; Psalm 139:13; Psalm 139:15b-16a; Psalm 139:14; and 1 Peter 2:4-5.

Have we fulfilled God's desire for us? No, but we haven't finished this journey. It's exciting to know that our Father will not allow us to stay like we are today. He has formed us in His image; therefore, it is possible to change and become like Him.

We are created to worship Him and give praises to Him. Yet, because man has a choice for life or death, decisions have been made wrongfully. But Jesus stands with His arms outstretched, waiting for a heart renewal and commitment of surrender from His children. When we trust Him with all our heart, and walk in His ways through obedience, we start to see a new life with character change. The mirror of self fades away and we begin to see a new picture in the frame of our life. The image of Christ starts to develop by Him showing us what He prophesied concerning our destiny.

Acts 17:28 (NKJV) says "for in Him we live and move and have our being," with the key words to this verse being, "in Him." When separated from the Vine, who is Jesus, spiritual growth and development—as He has designed—will end. We become nothing (see John 15:5).

We are wonderfully made, and marvelous are the works that He created for each soul to have and develop. You are His miraculous creation, and He wants you to walk in it!

Pappa God's Exhortation

I made no mistakes when I formed you in My image. I carefully developed your life with the talents and gifts that I imparted to you. You are no mistake. Wonderful and skillful and marvelous are you in My eyes of perfection. However, a sacrifice is required to become who I created. Only IN ME do you receive your true identity. Refuse to allow the enemy to steal away the blessings that I long to give as you become who I created. *~Pappa God*

1. What does God say about you and what did He mean by masterpiece? Explain.

2. If you were created in His perfection, why do you criticize who you are? Everyone dislikes something about themselves. What is your issue of being unsatisfied, and what are the dislikes about who you are? Explain.

3. Do you seek to be like others or one particular person (which is not so good, sometimes)? What is it that they have, that you don't? Have you asked God why?

4. Do you have a desire to look like Jesus? Are you seeking Him instead of others? When finding an area or areas, what would you do to start your healing journey?

5. With all the verses given in the Word about how God sees you, if you can't see these things, what do you think is the problem? Explain.

6. Do you trust God? Do you believe Him and His Word?

_____

_____

7. What was your relationship like between you and your earthly father?

_____

_____

8. Many times, broken and unhealthy earthly father relationships are the reasons for distrust and unbelief in God. Take time with your teacher, mentor, or pastor to discuss issues in your life that hinder you from accepting who you are in Him.

_____

_____

9. What did you learn from Pappa God's exhortation?

_____

_____

> "I am blameless, yet I do not know myself;
> I despise my life." (Job 9:21 NKJV)
>
> All things happen for the best for those who
> love God and walk in His will.

Notes of Reflection: _____

Chapter 28

The Christian Hypocrite (Part 1)

"For the leaders of this people cause them to err,
And those who are led by them are destroyed...
For everyone is a hypocrite and an evildoer,
And every mouth speaks folly."
(Isaiah 9:16 and 9:17b NKJV)

Hypocrisy is the practice of claiming to have moral standards or beliefs to which one's own behavior does not conform. Does that sound like you? It's ok, I said no also, but discovered later that one or two of my actions were on the list located in Part 2. Just because I identified with some of these actions, I would not have labeled myself as a hypocrite. But while I was preparing for this study, my eyes were opened to what the scriptures had to say. Here it is.

In the above scripture, Isaiah 9 verse 16, the Pharisees, who were the leaders, caused people to err. It was the blind leading the blind (Matthew 15:14). And those who were led by them would be destroyed by their lies. These people were hypocrites.

Jewish leaders—the Pharisees, or those not having a relationship with God—appeared to be leading, but led people astray. Christians today can be deceived and unaware that the emotions or characteristics of a hypocrite can lead others in the wrong direction. Surprisingly, verse 17b speaks of *everyone* being a hypocrite and evildoer, with a mouth that speaks folly.

Let's look at what Matthew 12:34 from the New Testament, says. "Brood of vipers! How can you, being evil, speak good things? For out of the abundance of the heart the mouth speaks" (NKJV).

Jesus refers to the hypocrites in the New Testament as *wolves in sheep's clothing.* Once again, they appeared to be something when they were not. Look at Job's friends: they liked pointing the finger and accusing him of sinning with a bitter-sweetness in their mouths. Their haughtiness and pride showed up with wrong accusations about Job. And his friends did not speak with correct and honorable words towards God. And God knew. He saw and heard the hearts of Job's accusers. Their actions were judgment and false words. However, Job's heart was different than his friends. And God was proud and honored to know and see Job's heart of love and integrity towards Him (Job 42:8).

Hypocritical actions or emotions could be the result of deep roots that have developed for several reasons. Past wounds may still cause bitterness, anger, and unforgiveness, while a struggle over lost identity is present. A need for deliverance around self-forgiveness and self-love could hinder future steps. Not realizing that accusations spoken are judgment, the finger we point is turned in our direction rather than in the direction of the victim.

God begins to alert us of our own faults, sins, and inabilities. Seeing the picture of a kitten instead of the strong lion in the mirror, we become aware of what others are seeing in our Christian walk.

A quote that I heard years ago stirs my heart daily: "Reasons are how we got to where we are but excuses keep us there!" This excuse is called *pride,* which is a form of hypocrisy, and its root can be deep and long.

As we seek Jesus, 1 John 1:6 (NKJV) gives us the answer we long for: "If we say that we have fellowship with Him, and walk in darkness, we lie and do not practice the truth." To claim that we belong to Him but then go out and live for ourselves is hypocrisy.

The hypocrite is one who acts a false part and has a false profession: a cheat, deceiver, dissembler, imposter, pretender. He hopes to prosper through ways which are not the ways of Christ. Nor does he have the character of Christ. The word *hypocrisy* is not found in the Fruit of the Spirit. It is not of God. This area of the flesh has not died if the actions of the hypocrite are still alive within.

Let's continue our lesson about The Christian Hypocrite, in the next chapter.

Pappa God's Exhortation

My children, I made you in My likeness; therefore, walk, talk, and live like Me. Why do you choose another way and walk in it while confessing Me as your Savior? You hypocrites! My Word is clear to understand and not hard to walk in if you genuinely love Me. I am light and in Me there is NO darkness. You can't serve two masters at once: you will love one and hate the other. I am the way, the truth, and the life. Choose life. *~Pappa God*

1. What is a hypocrite? What is a Christian hypocrite?

2. Have you ever thought that you may be on the list of the Christian hypocrite? How?

3. In the following chapter, you will find a small list. It may be surprising to some, but we are all on that list according to the verse in Isaiah. Have you checked those areas yet? Not pointing a finger, but it helps us to see where we stand in our character. Not so good, sometimes.

4. So, what can we do about it? Where would you start on your healing journey? Explain.

5. A good start is: what is your goal in life? Does it include Jesus?

6. If it doesn't include Jesus, why do you talk about Him being Lord? This is the first hypocritical statement—talking about who we are and walking a double-sided life.

7. Based on the previous chapters that we have discussed, what would be your next step in solving this problem?

8. Do those who you mingle with notice these things? Are they seeing a true relationship with Jesus or a hypocrite?

9. Do you think that these actions may deter them from making a commitment with Jesus? Why? Explain.

10. What did you learn from Pappa God's exhortation?

"For the eyes of the Lord are on the righteous, And His ears are open to their prayers; But the face of the Lord is against those who do evil." (1 Peter 3:12 NKJV)

Notes of Reflection: _____

The Christian Hypocrite (Part 2)

"Now the Spirit expressly says that in latter times
some will depart from the faith, giving heed to
deceiving spirits and doctrines of demons,
speaking lies in hypocrisy, having their own
conscience seared with a hot iron."
(1 Timothy 4:1-2 NKJV)

In the above verse, Timothy shares what the last days will be like. He warns and alerts us that these things are possible. Announcing that some will depart from the faith is not what the Christian wants to hear. Your faith, your walk with the Lord, could be in danger if you give in to deceiving spirits and doctrines of demons, while speaking lies of hypocrisy. Those who live by faith—believing that Jesus died for their sins—and put their trust in Christ, can be deceived and fall away. Hypocritical lies start to become a truth within, scarring their conscious—having no remorseful feelings toward sin as if seared with a hot iron. But how? In the second book of Timothy, he gives us an insight on how a believer's faith can be lost. Let's look deeper.

In these last days and perilous times, as 2 Timothy 3:1-5 explains, people will become ungodly more than usual. This verse unfolds these actions vividly of what their walk and character will become. Let's look at the list given to us in verses 2-5 (NKJV): "For men will be lovers of themselves, lovers of money, boasters, proud, blasphemers, disobedience to parents, unthankful, unholy, unloving, unforgiving, slanderers, without self-control, brutal, despisers of good, traitors, headstrong, haughty, lovers of pleasure rather than lovers of God, having a form of godliness but denying its power." These are all traits of a hypocrite if you proclaim to be a Christian. Why? They go against the ways of Christ.

So, Timothy sends a warning to be aware of how the enemy will steal, kill, and destroy. All these areas may not appear in everyone, but "everyone is a hypocrite" (see Isaiah 9:17b, from Part 1 of this teaching). If you engage in one hypocritical sin, you're guilty, but not necessarily of all. But the label of hypocrite may still hover over your head.

Here is a small list with scripture verses added. We must understand that an open door gives permission for the enemy to come in and make his kill. So, an open door to one is an open door to all:

1. Insincere repentance (Exodus 9:27)
2. Double-minded men (Psalm 119:113)
3. Detestable prayers of lawbreakers (Proverbs 28:9)
4. Meaningless oath (Isaiah 48:1)
5. Mockery fasting (Isaiah 58:4-5)
6. Holier than thou (Isaiah 65:4-5)
7. Judging others (Romans 2:1)
8. Lip service (Mark 7:6)
9. Saying things and doing another (Romans 2:21-24)
10. Social hypocrisy (Galatians 2:11-13)
11. Unbridled tongue (James 1:26)

Every one of these emotional and insecure characteristics is hypocrisy when the Christian continually practices them. As long as we wear this flesh suit, these or other emotions flare up in our lives. Although, when Christ came into our heart and became our advocate, the old man died and the new man took its place. But the soul—the mind, will, and emotions—must die for the new spirit-man to take over.

Prayer is needed for the one who walks in these ways. The soul is still wounded and broken in areas that are connected to these emotions. Just as we seek the grace and mercy from others when He continues to prune us, we need to extend the same to our brothers and sisters. The finger points both ways.

Pappa God's Exhortation

Although, I have created you in My image, the soul of your flesh must die to its ungodly ways. I have provided these ways through My Word; however, total commitment to Me only is required. Learning to walk, by allowing Me to prune away these fleshly ways, comes by keeping ungodly doors shut. If not, Satan has the permission to come in and destroy and kill. Receive this warning from the face in the mirror that is not Mine. I do not accept the two-faced or hypocrite in My kingdom. Seek holiness through My Son only.
~Pappa God

Chapter 29 Discussion and Teaching Questions

1. 1.Timothy 4:1-2, our chapter verse, says that many will fall from the faith in these latter days. Give details of why and how this will happen.

2. Men have been deceived from the beginning. Why is there more deception now than at the beginning? Explain.

3. Looking at the list, man is guilty of many, if not all of these things at some time in life. Can man turn his heart around and be changed?

4. If so, what would a person need to do? How would you go about this process? Explain.

5. Not to accuse you, but the question needs to be raised: are you making those changes in the areas that you have found hypocrisy in your life? How does God convict you about these areas in your life?

6. Do you think that these things are a part of the spots, wrinkles, and blemishes that linger within?

7. Could these issues that we are challenged with be connected to childhood traumas that have never been healed?

8. Could these be the little foxes that cripple you with fear, anger, bitterness, rejection, rebellion, etc.?

9. What did you learn from Pappa God's exhortation?

Insecurity within can create very unhealthy emotional characteristics. Deliverance may be needed along with weekly counseling and mentoring. If you think you may need to get more help in these areas, then don't waste time. Seek the Holy Spirit to direct you to the correct person.

> The word *hypocrite* comes from a Greek word that means "play actor." A hypocrite is someone pretending to be something that he or she is not in order to receive recognition or gain. Hypocrisy is a result of pride.

Notes of Reflection: _____

Chapter 30

It Doesn't Fit

"So Saul clothed David with his armor, and he put a
bronze helmet on his head; he also clothed him with a
coat of mail. David fastened his sword to his armor and
tried to walk, for he had not tested them. And David
said to Saul, 'I cannot walk with these, for I have not
tested them.' So, David took them off."
(1 Samuel 17:38-39 NKJV)

When David saw the weakness and fear of Saul's great and
fearless Philistine army, he stepped up to the plate ready to
fight. With David's small and tiny frame of a buffed man,
compared to the poised military men of strength, they laughed
at him. But David's courage and strength stood up, knowing
that this giant was no match for him!

Goliath challenged the Philistines to a fight, but after seeing
this huge mammoth of a man, the Philistines ducked their tail
and said, "No way are we going up against this giant." They
ran! This is when David volunteered for the assignment.

When Saul placed his armor on David, it was so large and
heavy that he couldn't even walk in it. So, David stepped out
in faith and prayed for guidance. Clothed in the armor of the
Lord, the breastplate of righteousness protected and shielded
him, while the helmet of salvation gave him confidence that
God was with him. His feet were shod with the gospel,
confirming that he was standing on the powerful Word of the
Lord. He knew that the belt of truth would set him free. David
equipped himself and stood and watched God move.

The ratings of Saul's career as a King, were poor. God was not pleased. The King was fearful, impatient, and prideful, and he was not a leader to the people. He lacked the qualifications, and his disobedience outweighed his obedience to God and Samuel.

Rebellion and rejection came from a wicked heart; therefore, God removed the anointing from his life. He was closing one door to open another.

Saul had proved himself to not be a leader through his disobedience and pride, and the lack of spiritual qualifications. With respect, David awaited his time in the wings of the stage that was set. But in this story, a spiritual nugget is given for us today: we can't expect to wear the armor of the enemy and win the battle of the Lord!

This famous biblical story about David teaches us that the clothing of evil/the enemy cannot be worn by the righteous. It doesn't fit! This is the reason why David could not wear Saul's armor for this battle. He couldn't mix good and evil. Saul's armor didn't fit because he was unrighteous, and David was a righteous man of God. David's weapon was not the sword, bats, or chains—it was pebble stones with a slingshot, anointed with power! This battle was orchestrated by God! David stepped out in faith, and with a powerful swing of his slingshot, he hit the giant in his forehead, sending him to the ground. Then, David took his sword and beheaded him.

This battle was won when David listened and obeyed God, not the world or ungodly people. It's time that we equip ourselves with the armor of God, and then we will see our battles won.

Pappa God's Exhortation

My children, your battles are already won in Me. Why do you expect to receive these victories being double-minded with the armor of evil attached? It will never be! I am light and in Me there is NO Darkness! Therefore, the clothes that you wear should be My garments that I have provided you with. Allow Me to strip this evil from you, if an expectation to be victorious in Me is desired. If you don't, nothing of Me you try to put on will fit! *~Pappa God*

1. Why can't you wear or put on just any kind of armor that you would like to, when you go into a spiritual battle?

2. Do you think that Goliath would have been killed if David wore Saul's armor? Why?

3. Knowing that the battle is not between flesh and blood but against the principalities and demons, what kind of spiritual weapon should be used? What kind of armor? Does this equipment "fit" anyone or just the man of God?

4. What did David speak out to Goliath before he swung his slingshot?

5. Should we speak out with our weapon toward the enemies that attack us? Why? What kind of words?

6. Do you put the armor of God on every day? If not, why not? Do you feel protected when you put on the armor of God?

7. Do you fear Satan? Why would you fear him if you are fully armed?

8. James tells us not to expect anything from God if we are being double-minded. Trying to fight a spiritual battle and living a double life, unstable in your walk, could hinder your victory; but by the grace of God, you could win. What is the difference between light and darkness? Explain.

9. Are you equipped to step out into spiritual battles now?

10. What did you learn from Pappa God's exhortation?

"For though we walk in the flesh, we do not war according to the flesh. For the weapons of our warfare are not carnal but mighty in God . . . " (2 Corinthians 10:3-4 NKJV)

You'll never win a battle if you've had a head experience instead of a heart experience."

Notes of Reflection: _____

About Shelia Humphries

$\mathbf{S}$helia Humphries is the founder and director of Restitution Ministries, in Ft. Worth, TX. In a previous ministry in Alabama, she ministered in state prisons, adult jails, juvenile facilities, the Women's Correctional Facility, and served in private invitational counseling and teaching. Her heart is to show the wounded that Jesus loves them regardless of their sin. Watching Jesus restore all that the enemy has stolen is the heart of this ministry.

Restitution Ministries brings forth the heart of God through teaching, discipleship, Bible study, and by helping *all* who need a touch of His love. Our vision and purpose is to see God's people succeed and become warriors for His Kingdom.

Let Restitution Ministries help equip you to fulfill your destiny in the Kingdom of God.

Contact Shelia by email at Shrestitution@yahoo.com.

Splendor Publishing

Splendor Publishing's life-changing books are written by skilled and passionate leaders, Christian ministers, entrepreneurs, and experts with a mission to make a positive impact in the lives of others.

Splendor books inspire and encourage personal, professional, and spiritual growth. For information about our book titles, authors, or publishing process, or for wholesale ordering for conferences, seminars, events, or training, visit SplendorPublishing.com.

Made in the USA
Monee, IL
09 November 2023

46113934R00115